SPECTRUM
Test Practice

Grade 8

Published by Spectrum
an imprint of Carson-Dellosa Publishing
Greensboro, NC

Editors: Jerry Aten and Stephanie Garcia

Spectrum
An imprint of Carson-Dellosa Publishing LLC
P.O. Box 35665
Greensboro, NC 27425 USA

ISBN 978-1-57768-978-2

06-304117784

SPECTRUM TEST PRACTICE
Table of Contents
Grade 8

Introduction 4
Letter to Parent/Guardian 7
Correlation to Standards.................................8

Reading
Vocabulary
Synonyms 11
Antonyms 12
Multi-Meaning Words 13
Words in Context..14
Sample Test: Vocabulary 15

Comprehension
Main Idea 17
Recalling Details 18
Inferences 19
Fact and Opinion..20
Story Elements 21
Nonfiction 22
Fiction 28
Sample Test: Reading Comprehension..........34
Reading Practice Test: Answer Sheet............39
Reading Practice Tests 40

Language
Mechanics
Punctuation 48
Capitalization and Punctuation 50
Sample Test: Language Mechanics 53

Language Expression
Usage...55
Sentences 58
Paragraphs 61
Sample Test: Language Expression...............65
Spelling 69
Sample Test: Spelling 71
Study Skills 73

Sample Test: Study Skills..............................77
Language Practice Test: Answer Sheet 79
Language Practice Test..................................80

Math
Concepts
Numeration..90
Number Concepts 93
Fractions & Decimals 96
Sample Test: Concepts 99

Computation
Operations on Whole Numbers.....................102
Operations on Decimals.................................104
Operations on Percents 106
Operations on Fractions.................................108
Sample Test: Computation 110

Applications
Geometry 113
Measurement 116
Problem Solving 118
Algebra..121
Sample Test: Applications 123
Math Practice Test: Answer Sheet 127
Math Practice Test..128

Science **134**
Sample Test: Science......................................139
Science Practice Test: Answer Sheet 141
Science Practice Test......................................142

Social Studies **144**
Sample Test: Social Studies..........................149
Social Studies Practice Test: Answer Sheet 151
Social Studies Practice Test..........................152

Answer Key 155

With increased accountability in ensuring academic success for all learners, testing now takes a significant amount of time for students in all settings. Standardized tests are designed to measure what students know. These tests are nationally normed. State tests are usually tied to specific academic standards identified for mastery.

For many students, testing can be a mystery. They fear not doing well and not knowing what to expect on the test. This *Spectrum Test Practice* book was developed to introduce students to both the format and the content they will encounter on tests. It was developed on the assumption that students have received prior instruction on the skills included. This book is designed to cover the content on a representative sample of state standards. The sampling of standards is found on pages 8–10 with a correlation to the skills covered in this book and a correlation to sample standardized tests. Spaces are provided to record the correlation to the tests being administered by the user of this book. Spaces are also provided to add standards that are specific to the user.

Features of *Spectrum Test Practice*

- Skill lessons, sample tests for subtopics, and comprehensive content area tests
- Clues for being successful with specific skills
- Correlation of skills to state standards and standardized tests
- Format and structure similar to other formal tests
- Written responses required in the science and social studies sections
- Reproducible for use by a teacher for a classroom

Overview

This book is developed within content areas (reading, language, math, science, and social studies). A comprehensive practice test follows at the end of each content area, with an answer sheet for students to record responses. Within each content area, specific subtopics have been identified. Sample tests are provided for each subtopic. Within each subtopic, specific skill lessons are presented. These specific skill lessons include an example and a clue for being successful with the skill.

Comprehensive Practice Test

A comprehensive practice test is provided for each content area. The subtopics for each area are identified below:

- **Reading**
  - Vocabulary (synonyms, antonyms, word meanings, multi-meaning words, root words, affixes, and words in context)
  - Reading comprehension (main idea, recalling details, sequencing, inferencing, drawing conclusions, fact and opinion, cause and effect, and author's purpose in fiction and nonfiction articles)

- **Language**
  - Language mechanics (capitalization and punctuation)
  - Language expression (usage, sentences, and paragraphs)
  - Spelling (both correct and incorrect spelling)
  - Study skills (dictionary skills, reference materials, reading tables and graphs, book parts)

- **Math**
  - Concepts (numeration, number concepts, fractions, and decimals)
  - Computation (operations on whole numbers, decimals, percents, and fractions)
  - Applications (geometry, measurement, problem solving, and algebra)
- **Science***
  - Earth science
  - Physical science
  - Life science
- **Social Studies***
  - United States geography
  - United States history
  - The Constitution
  - United States government
  - American Presidents

*Since states and often districts determine units of study within science and social studies, the content in this book may not be aligned with the content offered in all courses of study. The content within each area is grade level appropriate. It is based on a sampling of state standards. The tests in science and social studies include both multiple choice and written answer test items.

Comprehensive Practice Test Includes

- Content area (i.e., language)
- Subtopics (i.e., language mechanics)
- Directions, examples, and test questions
- Separate answer sheet with "bubbles" to be filled in for answers

Sample Tests

Sample tests are included for all subtopics.

These sample tests are designed to apply the knowledge and experience from the skill lessons in a more formal format. No clues are included. These sample tests are shorter than the comprehensive tests and longer than the skill lessons. The skills on the test items are presented in the same order as introduced in the book.

Sample Tests Include

- Subtopic (i.e., language mechanics)
- Directions, examples, and test questions

Skill Lessons

Skill lessons include sample questions and clues for mastering the skill. The questions are formatted as they generally appear in tests, whether the tests are standardized and nationally normed or state specific.

Skill Lessons Include

- Subtopic (i.e., language mechanics)
- Skill (i.e., punctuation)
- Directions and examples
- Clues for completing the activity
- Practice questions

Use

This book can be used in a variety of ways, depending on the needs of the students. Some examples follow:

- Review the skills correlation on pages 8–10. Record the skills tested in your state and/or district on the blanks provided.
- Administer the comprehensive practice test for each content area. Have students use the sample answer sheet in order to simulate the actual testing experience. The tests for reading, language, and math are multiple choice. Evaluate the results.

- Administer the sample test for the subtopics within the content area. Evaluate the results.

- Administer the specific skill lessons for those students needing additional practice with content. Evaluate the results.

- Use the skill lessons as independent work in centers, for homework, or as seatwork.

- Prepare an overhead transparency of skill lessons to be presented to a group of students. Use the transparency to model the skill and provide guided practice.

- Send home the Letter to Parent/Guardian found on page 7.

Clues for Getting Started

- Determine the structure for implementing *Spectrum Test Practice*. These questions may help guide you:

  - Do you want to assess the overall performance of your class in each academic area? If so, reproduce the test practice and sample answer sheet for each area. Use the results to determine subtopics that need additional instruction and/or practice.

  - Do you already have information about the overall achievement of your students within each academic area? Do you need more information about their achievement within subtopics, such as vocabulary within reading? If so, reproduce the sample tests for the subtopics.

  - Do your students need additional practice with some of the specific skills that they will encounter on the standardized test? Do you need to know which students have mastered which skills? These skill lessons provide opportunities for instruction and practice.

- Go over the purpose of tests with your students. Describe the tests and the testing situation, explaining that the tests are often timed, that answers are recorded on a separate answer sheet, and that the questions cover material they have studied.

- Do some of the skill lessons together to help students develop strategies for selecting answers and for different types of questions. Use the "clues" for learning strategies for test taking.

- Make certain that students know how to mark a separate answer sheet. Use the practice test and answer sheet so that they are familiar with the process.

- Review the directions for each test. Identify key words that students must use to answer the questions. Do the sample test questions with the class.

- Remind students to answer each question, to budget their time so they can complete all the questions, and to apply strategies for determining answers.

Reduce the mystery of taking tests for your students. By using *Spectrum Test Practice*, you have the materials that show them what the tests will look like, what kinds of questions are on the tests, and ways to help them be more successful taking tests.

Note: The reading comprehension questions in all selections are in the same order: main idea, recalling details/sequencing, inferencing/drawing conclusions, fact and opinion/cause and effect. This information can be used to diagnose areas for needed instruction.

Note: If you wish to time your students on a practice test, we suggest allowing 1.17 minutes per question for this grade level.

Dear Parent/Guardian:

We will be giving tests to measure your child's learning. These tests include questions that relate to the information your child is learning in school. The tests may be standardized and used throughout the nation, or they may be specific to our state. Regardless of the test, the results are used to measure student achievement.

Many students do not test well even though they know the material. They may not test well because of test anxiety or the mystery of taking tests. What will the test look like? What will some of the questions be? What happens if I do not do well?

To help your child do his/her best on the tests, we will be using some practice tests. These tests help your child learn what the tests will look like, what some of the questions might be, and ways to learn to take tests. These practice tests will be included as part of your child's homework.

You can help your child with this important part of learning. Below are some suggestions:

- Ask your child if he/she has homework.
- Provide a quiet place to work.
- Go over the work with your child.
- Use a timer to help your child learn to manage his/her time when taking tests.
- Tell your child he/she is doing a good job.
- Remind him/her to use the clues that are included in the lessons.

If your child is having difficulty with the tests, these ideas may be helpful:

- Review the examples.
- Skip the difficult questions and come back to them later.
- Guess at those that you do not know.
- Answer all the questions.

By showing you are interested in how your child is doing, he/she will do even better in school. Enjoy this time with your child. Good luck with the practice tests.

Sincerely,

● Grade 8

Sample Standards	Spectrum Test Practice Gr. 8	*CAT Level for Gr. 8	**CTBS Level for Gr. 8	Other	Other	Other
Reading						
Vocabulary						
Understanding Figurative Language						
Using Common Foreign Words						
Using Context Clues	X	X	X			
Using Synonyms and Antonyms	X	X	X			
Using Multi-Meaning Words	X		X			
Using Common Roots and Word Parts						
Other						
Comprehension						
Identifying Main Idea	X	X	X			
Using Graphic Organizers						
Comparing and Contrasting	X	X				
Reading Various Genre	X	X	X			
Summarizing	X	X	X			
Using Popular Media	X	X	X			
Identifying Author's Purpose	X	X	X			
Distinguishing Between Fact and Opinion	X		X			
Identifying Character Traits/Feelings	X	X	X			
Identifying Supporting Details	X	X	X			
Understanding Literary Devices	X	X	X			
Understanding Themes	X	X	X			
Drawing Conclusions	X	X	X			
Using Context Clues	X	X	X			
Analyzing Characterization	X	X	X			
Other						
Other						
Language						
Mechanics						
Expression						
Using Graphic Organizers						
Understanding Purpose		X				
Using Topic Sentences	X	X	X			
Using Supporting Sentences for Paragraphs	X	X	X			
Drawing Logical Conclusions	X	X	X			
Using Technology						
Using Editing Skills	X					
Using Different Types of Writing	X	X	X			
Using Simple, Compound, and Complex Sentences	X	X	X			
Using Proper Grammar	X	X	X			
Using Correct Capitalization and Punctuation	X	X	X			
Other						
Other						

* Terra Nova CAT™ ©2001 CTB/McGraw-Hill
** Terra Nova CTBS® ©1997 CTB/McGraw-Hill

Grade 8

Sample Standards	Spectrum Test Practice Gr. 8	*CAT Level for Gr. 8	**CTBS Level for Gr. 8	Other	Other	Other
Study Skills						
Using Reference Materials	X		X			
Other						
Math						
Concepts						
Numeration						
Comparing and Ordering Positive and Negative Integers	X		X			
Comparing and Ordering Fractions, Decimals, Percents	X					
Using Number Lines	X		X			
Using Scientific Notation and Square Roots	X	X	X			
Using Prime Factorization	X		X			
Recognizing Decimal-Fraction Equivalents	X					
Using Models	X	X				
Understanding Place Value	X	X	X			
Understanding Negative Integer Exponents						
Using Expressions			X			
Other						
Other						
Computation						
Using Operations on Positive and Negative Numbers	X		X			
Using Operations on Fractions, Decimals, Percents	X	X	X			
Using Rounding of Numbers	X					
Calculating Simple and Compound Interest						
Using Estimation	X	X	X			
Using Mental Arithmetic						
Using Appropriate Operations	X	X	X			
Other						
Other						
Algebra and Functions						
Solving Linear Equations with One Variable	X	X				
Solving Linear Equations with Two Variables	X		X			
Finding Slope of Linear Functions						
Using Graphs	X	X	X			
Other						
Other						
Geometry						
Understanding Coordinate Graphs	X		X			
Using the Pythagorean Theorem						
Using Transformations of Shapes	X		X			
Identifying Properties of 3-D Objects	X	X	X			
Finding/Comparing Area, Perimeter, and Volume	X	X	X			
Other						
Other						

* Terra Nova CAT™ ©2001 CTB/McGraw-Hill
** Terra Nova CTBS® ©1997 CTB/McGraw-Hill

9

Sample Standards	Spectrum Test Practice Gr. 8	*CAT Level for Gr. 8	**CTBS Level for Gr. 8	Other	Other	Other
Measurement						
Converting Common Measurements	x					
Comparing Different Units of Measure	x		x			
Calculating Circumference						
Calculating Amounts of Money	x	x	x			
Other						
Data Analysis						
Probability						
Analyzing Data in a Variety of Graphs	x	x	x			
Using Data to Predict Future Events	x	x	x			
Identifying Different Methods for Selecting Samples						
Other						
Problem Solving						
Using Strategies to Solve Problems	x	x	x			
Estimating Results						
Recognizing Reasonable Solutions			x			
Identifying Relevant Information	x		x			
Other						
Science						
Understanding the Composition of the Earth		x	x			
Understanding the Sun		x	x			
Understanding Matter and Energy	x	x	x			
Understanding Systems		x	x			
Understanding Organisms	x	x	x			
Other						
Social Studies						
History						
Understanding the American Revolution	x	x	x			
Understanding the National Expansion and Reform	x	x	x			
Understanding the Civil War	x	x	x			
Government						
Understanding Constitutional Government	x	x	x			
Other						
Economics						
Identifying Three Types of Economic Systems						
Understanding the Basic Economic Functions of the Government		x				
Understanding Savings and Investments						
Other						
Geography						
Interpreting Topographic Maps		x				
Locating All of the States on a United States Map						
Other						

* Terra Nova CAT™ ©2001 CTB/McGraw-Hill
** Terra Nova CTBS® ©1997 CTB/McGraw-Hill

Name _____ Date _____

READING: VOCABULARY

● Lesson 1: Synonyms

Directions: Read each question carefully. Fill in the circle of the word that means the same or about the same as the underlined word.

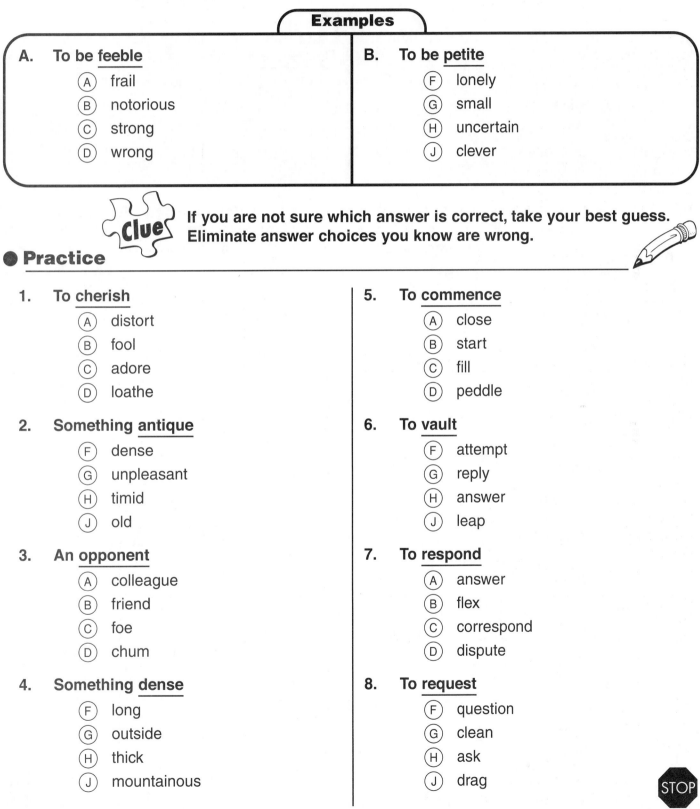

Examples

A. To be <u>feeble</u>
- (A) frail
- (B) notorious
- (C) strong
- (D) wrong

B. To be <u>petite</u>
- (F) lonely
- (G) small
- (H) uncertain
- (J) clever

Clue If you are not sure which answer is correct, take your best guess. Eliminate answer choices you know are wrong.

● Practice

1. To <u>cherish</u>
   - (A) distort
   - (B) fool
   - (C) adore
   - (D) loathe

2. Something <u>antique</u>
   - (F) dense
   - (G) unpleasant
   - (H) timid
   - (J) old

3. An <u>opponent</u>
   - (A) colleague
   - (B) friend
   - (C) foe
   - (D) chum

4. Something <u>dense</u>
   - (F) long
   - (G) outside
   - (H) thick
   - (J) mountainous

5. To <u>commence</u>
   - (A) close
   - (B) start
   - (C) fill
   - (D) peddle

6. To <u>vault</u>
   - (F) attempt
   - (G) reply
   - (H) answer
   - (J) leap

7. To <u>respond</u>
   - (A) answer
   - (B) flex
   - (C) correspond
   - (D) dispute

8. To <u>request</u>
   - (F) question
   - (G) clean
   - (H) ask
   - (J) drag

STOP

Name _____   Date_____

READING: VOCABULARY

● **Lesson 2: Antonyms**

Directions: Read each item carefully. Fill in the circle that corresponds to the word that means the opposite of the underlined word.

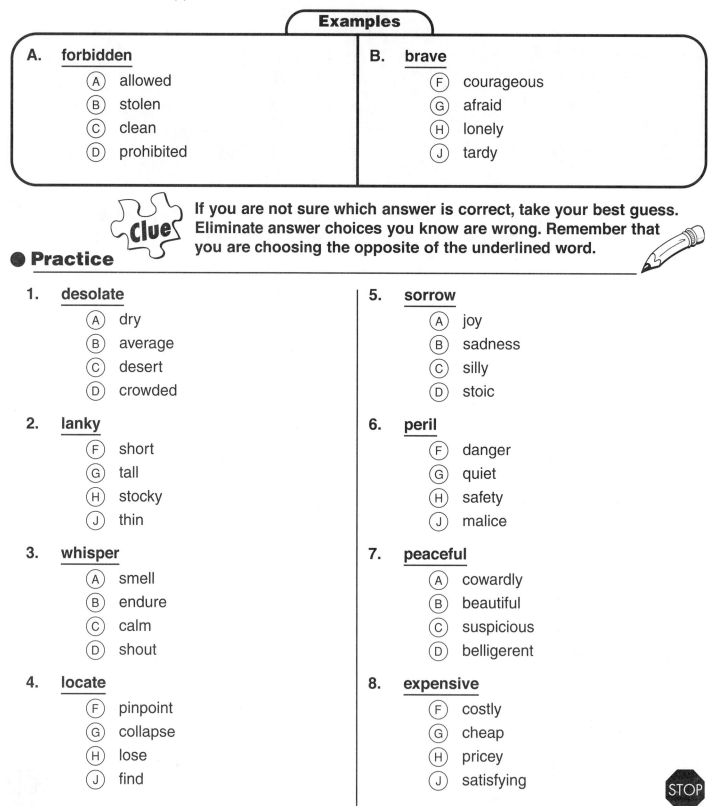

Examples

A. forbidden
- (A) allowed
- (B) stolen
- (C) clean
- (D) prohibited

B. brave
- (F) courageous
- (G) afraid
- (H) lonely
- (J) tardy

Clue If you are not sure which answer is correct, take your best guess. Eliminate answer choices you know are wrong. Remember that you are choosing the opposite of the underlined word.

● **Practice**

1. desolate
- (A) dry
- (B) average
- (C) desert
- (D) crowded

2. lanky
- (F) short
- (G) tall
- (H) stocky
- (J) thin

3. whisper
- (A) smell
- (B) endure
- (C) calm
- (D) shout

4. locate
- (F) pinpoint
- (G) collapse
- (H) lose
- (J) find

5. sorrow
- (A) joy
- (B) sadness
- (C) silly
- (D) stoic

6. peril
- (F) danger
- (G) quiet
- (H) safety
- (J) malice

7. peaceful
- (A) cowardly
- (B) beautiful
- (C) suspicious
- (D) belligerent

8. expensive
- (F) costly
- (G) cheap
- (H) pricey
- (J) satisfying

STOP

READING: VOCABULARY

● Lesson 3: Multi-Meaning Words

Directions: Read each item carefully. Fill in the circle that corresponds to the answer that fits best in both sentences.

Examples

A. When will the bell ___ to end this class? Carmen received a ___ for Christmas.

- (A) ring
- (B) invitation
- (C) shirt
- (D) sound

B. The Congressman hired a new ___. A ___ is missing from the book.

- (F) summons
- (G) call
- (H) page
- (J) pass

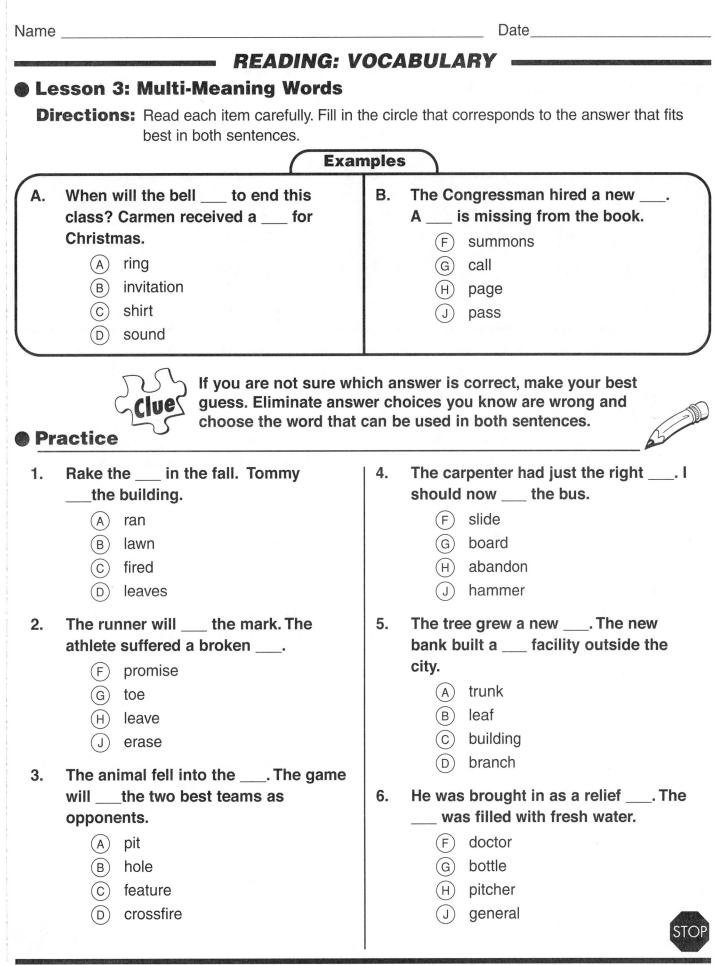

Clue If you are not sure which answer is correct, make your best guess. Eliminate answer choices you know are wrong and choose the word that can be used in both sentences.

● Practice

1. Rake the ___ in the fall. Tommy ___the building.
   - (A) ran
   - (B) lawn
   - (C) fired
   - (D) leaves

2. The runner will ___ the mark. The athlete suffered a broken ___.
   - (F) promise
   - (G) toe
   - (H) leave
   - (J) erase

3. The animal fell into the ___. The game will ___the two best teams as opponents.
   - (A) pit
   - (B) hole
   - (C) feature
   - (D) crossfire

4. The carpenter had just the right ___. I should now ___ the bus.
   - (F) slide
   - (G) board
   - (H) abandon
   - (J) hammer

5. The tree grew a new ___. The new bank built a ___ facility outside the city.
   - (A) trunk
   - (B) leaf
   - (C) building
   - (D) branch

6. He was brought in as a relief ___. The ___ was filled with fresh water.
   - (F) doctor
   - (G) bottle
   - (H) pitcher
   - (J) general

STOP

READING: VOCABULARY

● Lesson 4: Words in Context

Directions: Read each sentence carefully. Look for a clue in each of the sentences that will help you to decide the word that will be the best choice to fill in the blank.

Examples

A. Pack ___ pairs of socks. You will need a fresh pair every day.
- Ⓐ warm
- Ⓑ numerous
- Ⓒ clean
- Ⓓ wool

B. A rich man gives. A ___ organization receives.
- Ⓕ needy
- Ⓖ unhealthy
- Ⓗ common
- Ⓙ professional

Clue Skim each sentence. Use the meaning of what you read to find the right choice. If necessary, try substituting each answer choice in the blank.

● Practice

1. Because the knife was dull, I had to ___ the blade.
   - Ⓐ burn
   - Ⓑ carry
   - Ⓒ sharpen
   - Ⓓ roll

2. For lunch I had a slice of ___ and a roast beef sandwich.
   - Ⓕ life
   - Ⓖ haddock
   - Ⓗ melon
   - Ⓙ caution

3. I was ___ of my father's decision by telephone.
   - Ⓐ refrained
   - Ⓑ denied
   - Ⓒ alarmed
   - Ⓓ informed

4. Tom's family was most impressed with the ___ setting of the cabin in the forest.
   - Ⓕ tranquil
   - Ⓖ warlike
   - Ⓗ everyday
   - Ⓙ expensive

5. A stoplight was installed at the ___ of Grant and Columbus.
   - Ⓐ rescinded
   - Ⓑ intersection
   - Ⓒ plantation
   - Ⓓ painting

6. Samuel, the ___ of the family, paid for everyone's dinner.
   - Ⓕ patrician
   - Ⓖ patron
   - Ⓗ partnership
   - Ⓙ patriarch

STOP

READING: VOCABULARY
SAMPLE TEST

● **Directions:** Read each item carefully.

Examples

For Example A, choose the word that correctly completes both sentences.

A.   Tim seems to have good ___. Birds can ___ a storm.
- (A) judgment
- (B) feel
- (C) sense
- (D) reasoning

For Example B, choose the word that means the opposite of the underlined word.

B.   inevitable situation
- (F) avoidable
- (G) confusing
- (H) stressful
- (J) enjoyable

For numbers 1–8, find the word or words that mean the same or almost the same as the underlined word.

1.   surprise verdict
- (A) question
- (B) decision
- (C) unusual
- (D) investment

2.   somber moment
- (F) passing
- (G) fleeting
- (H) bleak
- (J) joyful

3.   recollect the past
- (A) forget
- (B) ignore
- (C) remember
- (D) separate

4.   plentiful supply
- (F) abundant
- (G) scarce
- (H) fresh
- (J) rationed

5.   irritate the teacher
- (A) accommodate
- (B) irk
- (C) pacify
- (D) moderate

6.   deter others
- (F) encourage
- (G) follow
- (H) satisfy
- (J) discourage

7.   brief statement
- (A) lengthy
- (B) concise
- (C) hollow
- (D) untrue

8.   improper behavior
- (F) attitude
- (G) conduct
- (H) experience
- (J) useful

GO ON

Name _____   Date_____

For numbers 9–12, find the word that means the opposite of the underlined word.

9. feel **enmity**
   - (A) disappoint
   - (B) friendship
   - (C) impatience
   - (D) relief

10. **ignite** a fire
    - (F) extinguish
    - (G) observe
    - (H) light
    - (J) approach

11. **cancel** the subscription
    - (A) erase
    - (B) confirm
    - (C) eliminate
    - (D) hire

12. deep **despair**
    - (F) depression
    - (G) application
    - (H) maintenance
    - (J) optimism

For numbers 13–16, read each item and decide on the best choice for the blank space by using the clues in each statement.

13. He keeps a ___ of candy in his locker.
    - (A) locker
    - (B) hoard
    - (C) shelter
    - (D) racket

14. A rich but ___ man.
    - (F) humble
    - (G) wealthy
    - (H) poor
    - (J) prosperous

15. Gold is a ___ metal.
    - (A) canister
    - (B) rich
    - (C) hard
    - (D) precious

16. The school uniform was the correct ___.
    - (F) code
    - (G) attire
    - (H) response
    - (J) racket

For numbers 17–18, choose the word that correctly completes both sentences.

17. The ___ led to their freedom from rule by England. The tire made one complete ___.
    - (A) handsome
    - (B) insurance
    - (C) revolution
    - (D) talk

18. Soup is cooking on the ___. Out west, cattle roam the open ___.
    - (F) range
    - (G) prairie
    - (H) plains
    - (J) stove

STOP

READING: COMPREHENSION

● **Lesson 5: Main Idea**

Directions: Read each item carefully. Then choose the correct answer and the circle that corresponds to that choice.

Example

Tyler wanted a new cell phone to take with him to college. His father bought him one but told Tyler that he would have to pay for any extra minutes that were not included in the monthly charge.

A.   **The message in the passage for Tyler is**

ⓐ   Buy the phone yourself.

ⓑ   Tell your friends not to call.

ⓒ   Keep track of the minutes that have been used each month.

ⓓ   Confusion is a big issue here.

Skim the passage and then answer the questions. Refer back to the passage to find the answers. You don't have to reread the passage for each question.

● **Practice**

A Childhood Promise

In a sandy cotton field in Georgia, a boy stood up. He looked at his bleeding hands. The cotton bolls had sliced his hands, but he wasn't thinking about the cuts. He was imagining different landscapes, like the ones his uncle had seen during his travels in the Navy. The boy promised himself that one day he would enlist in the Navy. He vowed that he would go to college, too, even though none of his family had ever attended college. That boy was James E. Carter, better known as Jimmy, and he would grow up to become president of the United States.

That boy achieved all he had set out to achieve, plus much he could not have imagined for himself. Through it all, he never forgot what it was like to live among desperately poor people. Instead of isolating himself from the poverty that had surrounded him as a child, he attacked the causes of poverty. Perhaps the example he provides is his greatest accomplishment.

1.   **What is the main idea of this reading?**

ⓐ   Getting to know Jimmy Carter

ⓑ   Jimmy Carter was determined to someday enroll in the Navy and go to college.

ⓒ   The days following Jimmy Carter's presidency

ⓓ   The perils of picking cotton

2.   **Which of these statements supports the main idea of the article?**

Ⓕ   Cotton bolls are very sharp.

Ⓖ   Carter enrolled in the U.S. Naval Academy, where he studied nuclear physics.

Ⓗ   Cotton plants need irrigation.

Ⓙ   Jimmy Carter always wanted to become president.

3.   **Which would be another good title for this reading?**

ⓐ   Jimmy's Vow

ⓑ   Path to the Presidency

ⓒ   Poverty in Georgia

ⓓ   From Rags to Riches

STOP

READING: COMPREHENSION

● Lesson 6: Recalling Details

Directions: Read each item carefully. Then choose the correct answer that corresponds to that choice.

Example

While the fire was probably a case of arson, the investigator could not seem to find all of the evidence he needed to connect the main suspect to the scene of the fire. In the end it was the suspect himself who provided the missing link to the crime.

A. **How was this case of arson finally solved?**

- (A) Due to the diligence of the investigator
- (B) Due to the suspect's own mistakes
- (C) A stroke of genius
- (D) The time of day confirmed the fire.

 Clue Skim the passage and then answer the questions. Refer back to the passage to find the answers. You don't have to reread the passage for each question.

● Practice

Fire Mystery

Oily rags packed tightly into a box or a silo filled with damp grain suddenly bursting into flames appear to be mysterious, for they have no apparent causes. But there is one cause of fire that many people don't understand or even think about — spontaneous combustion.

All fires are caused by the heat that is given off when oxygen combines with some material. Fast oxidation gives off much heat and light very quickly and causes things to burn. Slow oxidation gives off no light and very little heat, not nearly enough to cause a fire. But when this little bit of heat is trapped it can not escape into the air. Instead it builds up. As more and more oxidation occurs, more heat is trapped. As the material gets hotter it oxidizes faster, and the faster oxidation produces even more heat. Finally things get so hot that a fire starts. Damp or oily materials and powdery substances are the most likely things to produce spontaneous combustion because a little moisture makes them oxidize more quickly.

1. **Which of these materials is most likely to produce spontaneous combustion?**
   - (A) wood
   - (B) oily rags
   - (C) aluminum foil
   - (D) hot rocks

2. **Which of these is not good advice for storing combustible materials?**
   - (F) tightly packed box
   - (G) loosely packed box
   - (H) stored only when completely dry
   - (J) stored in open containers

3. **Which is the best description of spontaneous combustion?**
   - (A) oxygen combining with some material
   - (B) no light and little heat given off
   - (C) materials get so hot they explode into flames
   - (D) much heat and some light

 STOP

Name _____ Date_____

READING: COMPREHENSION

● Lesson 7: Inferences

Directions: Read each item. Choose the best answer and fill in the circle that corresponds to that choice.

Example

Ray stayed after school to finish some research he needed from the library. He missed the bus and now he needs to find a way home. He tries to call his older brother on his cell phone, but Randy's phone is not turned on. After quickly considering his options, Ray decides his best option is the following:

A.
- (A) Call his father at work and ask him to pick him up at school on the way home.
- (B) Even though the walk is over seven miles, he probably should start walking.
- (C) He should go through the building looking for a teacher who might be headed his way.
- (D) He should plan on spending the night at school.

Clue Skim the passage. Then read the questions. Refer back to the passage to find the answers. You don't have to reread the passage for each question.

● Practice

A Letter Home

Dear Mom,

I would have written sooner, but we have been busy. If you have been able to go to the movies, you probably saw it all on the Movietone newsreels.

How was Thanksgiving? Did Uncle Aubrey have enough gas rations to come? Our cooks did a good job here. All day long, I was sniffing all those good smells coming from the galley. We had sausage dressing, though, and not your special cornbread dressing. How is my sister? I can't believe that a year ago the two of us were leaving the house together and walking the railroad tracks to high school. Tell her, if she sees Betty at school to tell her Ray was thinking about her.

1. **Which of these ages do you think comes closest to Ray's age when he wrote the letter?**
   - (A) 15
   - (B) 17
   - (C) 19
   - (D) 29

2. **During which of these time periods do you think it is most probable that this letter was composed?**
   - (F) The Great Depression
   - (G) World War II
   - (H) Vietnam War
   - (J) Desert Storm

STOP

READING: COMPREHENSION

● Lesson 8: Fact and Opinion

Directions: Read each item carefully. Then choose the correct answer and fill in the circle that corresponds to that choice.

Examples

The Constitutional Convention met with the idea of revising the Articles of Confederation. There were many disagreements between the large and small states concerning the balance of power. In the end it was decided to create an entirely new document that would satisfy both sides.

A. **Which of the following is not a fact?**

- Ⓐ There were disagreements between the small and large states.
- Ⓑ A Constitutional Committee did meet.
- Ⓒ The Articles of Confederation had no value whatsoever.
- Ⓓ The Articles of Confederation had been the framework of the government.

Clue Skim the passage and then answer the questions. Refer back to the passage to find the answers. You don't have to reread the passage for each question.

● Practice

Young Inventors

If you are learning to play the guitar, you might have reason to thank Nicholas Ravagni. Ravagni owns a patent that helps new guitar players figure out where to place their fingers. Ravagni obtained his patent when he was 11. He got the idea for his invention when he was only six. He designed a self-adhesive and color-coded strip of plastic that fits under a guitar's strings.

You can thank other young inventors for everyday products. Open your refrigerator. You can probably find leftovers wrapped in aluminum foil. Thank Charles Hall, a college student who began experimenting with a process to create a cheap and ready supply of aluminum. When you tune in to your favorite FM radio station, thank Edwin Armstrong. Just after the turn of the century, Armstrong read a book about inventions.

Only 15, he decided that he would become an inventor of radios. By the time he was in his early twenties, he had made discoveries that would lead to his development of the FM radio.

1. **Which of the following is a fact?**

- Ⓐ Edwin Armstrong's inventions were more important than those of Charles Hall.
- Ⓑ Hall and Armstrong would advise children to have faith in their own abilities.
- Ⓒ Hall should have gotten better grades when he was in college.
- Ⓓ Ravagni was the youngest of these inventors to obtain his first patent.

READING: COMPREHENSION

● **Lesson 9: Story Elements**

Directions: Read each item carefully. Then choose the correct answer and fill in the circle that corresponds to that choice.

Example

When the two boys reached the mouth of the cave, Tommy told Mike that he would need a flashlight. "Rats!" Mike exclaimed. "I left mine in my backpack."

A. The setting for this story is
- (A) Tommy and Mike
- (B) The mouth of the cave
- (C) The forgotten flashlight
- (D) Mike's backpack

● **Practice**

Skim the passage. Then answer the questions. Refer back to the passage to find the answers. You don't have to reread the passage for each question.

I Wasn't So Sure!

Mom said the smell of a summer morning from the ground up was worth all the ants that shared your food, but I wasn't so sure. She said that the wilderness would teach a boy how to make decisions like a man. I thought she was being silly. Funny how you get surprised.

It was my fault. One of those manly choices, when all I wanted to be was a little boy. All I could think about was swimming. I didn't want to pick the tent spot. So when I found one with just a few mounds of dirt I stomped down the mounds and was swimming in no time. It wasn't until later that we met our tent mates. I climbed into my sleeping bag. I ignored the first few bites, kicking whatever was at the bottom of my bag. Shortly, Mom crawled into her bag. I heard her kick the bottom of her sleeping bag too. Soon I heard her roll over and slap her arm.

"What is in these bags?" she demanded. "I'm getting eaten alive." I switched on the flashlight, aiming it at her bag. Swarming in the light's circular glow were hundreds of tiny red ants.

Mom said, "I think you found an ant hill!" She grabbed her keys and headed for the car. Now, I'm more careful when I pick a tent site.

1. The setting for this story is a—
- (A) river.
- (B) scout camp.
- (C) lake.
- (D) beach.

2. What is the main reason for his mother coming along on the camping trip?
- (F) to tuck him in at night
- (G) to help him learn how to become a man by making decisions in the wilderness
- (H) to drive him
- (J) to cook his food

3. Which offers the best lesson learned by the main character?
- (A) to make good decisions
- (B) to stay in a motel
- (C) to bring along ant spray
- (D) to trust his mother

READING: COMPREHENSION

● Lesson 10: Nonfiction

Directions: Read each item carefully. Then choose the correct answer and fill in the circle that corresponds to that choice.

Examples

Many of our great presidents are recognized for their deeds by placing their faces on U.S. coins. While President Lincoln is depicted on a penny, Thomas Jefferson's face is on a nickel. President Roosevelt's face is on a dime and the face of George Washington is found on quarters.

A. **This passage is about**
- Ⓐ The value of having presidents on coins
- Ⓑ The importance of George Washington
- Ⓒ The presidents whose faces appear on coins
- Ⓓ The value of collecting coins

Clue Here is a story about a man who loved adventure. Read the story and then answer questions 1 through 7.

● Practice

Conquering Everest

Edmund Hillary first discovered mountain climbing on a school field trip. He loved climbing right away and would climb the local mountains at every opportunity. To climb safely, a person must be strong and reliable; Edmund was both. By the time he was in his twenties, Edmund was recognized for his mountaineering talents and had mastered many difficult feats. The young climber then decided to try some mountains in Europe. Through his adventures there, Edmund met Sir John Hunt, who was planning an expedition to Mount Everest. Situated on the border of Nepal and Tibet, the 29,028-foot-high peak had never been climbed successfully. Hunt quickly invited Edmund to go along on the trip, and the result was history. On May 29, 1953, Edmund and his Nepalese guide, Tenzing Norgay, were the first

people to reach the summit of the world's tallest mountain.

Edmund was responsible for setting up supply areas around the South Pole. To do this, he drove farm tractors to the supply sites and left the food and fuel behind. When he had finished the deliveries he drove all the way to the South Pole. Edmund's skilled management of the assignment helped the team attain its goal.

For the next twenty years Edmund continued to climb in the Himalayas. During this time, he came to know and depend on the Sherpas, the Nepalese people. Edmund's concern and appreciation for the Sherpas was so great that he raised money to build schools and hospitals for them, even helping with the construction.

GO ON

READING COMPREHENSION

● Lesson 10: Nonfiction (cont.)

Because of his many accomplishments and his dedication to human and environmental rights, Edmund received honorary degrees and decorations. He was also knighted in 1953. Sir Edmund Hillary accomplished much in his life. He is important not only because of his outdoor achievements, but because of his dedication to the things he believed in.

1. This excerpt is mostly about a person who—

Ⓐ had dreams of becoming famous.

Ⓑ fought his way out of poverty.

Ⓒ was able to succeed despite many handicaps.

Ⓓ achieved greatness in several arenas.

2. Who accompanied Sir Edmund Hillary on his most famous climb?

Ⓕ Sir Vivian Fuchs

Ⓖ a Hindu guide

Ⓗ a Nepalese guide

Ⓙ no one—he did it alone

3. According to what you read, which of these statements would Sir Edmund Hillary probably support?

Ⓐ We should explore nature responsibly.

Ⓑ People have the right to use nature as they wish.

Ⓒ It is more important to take than to give.

Ⓓ If you think you can't do something, don't try to do it.

4. Which is an opinion?

Ⓕ Hillary was the greatest mountain climber ever.

Ⓖ Hillary scaled Mt. Everest.

Ⓗ Hillary was knighted.

Ⓙ Mt. Everest is on the border of Nepal and Tibet.

5. While Hillary enjoyed adventures all over the earth, the scene of his greatest achievement was probably—

Ⓐ Mt. Everest.

Ⓑ the Amazon River.

Ⓒ Mt. Lemmon.

Ⓓ the Andes Mountains.

6. The word *decorations*, as it is used in the paragraph, probably means—

Ⓕ ways to make a place look nice.

Ⓖ awards or honors.

Ⓗ ribbons and bows.

Ⓙ lights and ornaments.

7. Choose the answer that best explains why Hillary built schools and hospitals for the Sherpas.

Ⓐ It was part of his job as high commissioner.

Ⓑ He wanted to prove that he could build things.

Ⓒ He wanted to do something for them.

Ⓓ He did it so they would keep helping him.

READING: COMPREHENSION

● **Lesson 11: Nonfiction**

Directions: Read each item carefully. Then choose the correct answer and fill in the circle that corresponds to that choice.

Example

The waffle cone was an invention of chance. During a fair in St. Louis, an ice cream vendor ran out of the paper bowls he was using to serve the ice cream. In the booth next to his was a vendor selling sweet pastries cooked on a waffle iron. The ice cream man bought some of the waffles and began serving ice cream in them. The waffle cone was born.

A. This passage was all about—

  (A) the invention of ice cream.
  (B) the birth of the waffle cone.
  (C) a cold treat at the fair.
  (D) the first ice cream sundae.

Clue Skim the passage. Then answer the questions. Refer back to the passage to find the answers. You don't have to reread the story for each question.

● **Practice**

Tent Canvas Turned Overalls

In the mid-1800s, two chance events occurred in the life of a young "gold rusher" that resulted in the creation of the world's first pair of jeans. Twenty-three-year-old Levi Strauss, a Bavarian immigrant working at his brothers' dry goods store in New York City, did not join the gold rush because he wanted to stake a claim. He wanted to sell supplies to the men and women who did.

So in January of 1853, Levi Strauss acquired a waterfront building in San Francisco and began selling dry goods and Strauss Brothers products as his brothers' West Coast distributor. Business went well for him. Strauss ran an honest operation and became a wealthy and well-respected man.

Then the first chance occurrence that led to the availability of jeans presented itself to Levi. Mr. Strauss imagined that the gold miners he catered to would require denim canvas with which to build tents and cover Conestoga wagons. He was wrong. Pleasant California weather persuaded miners to sleep directly under the stars. Levi would have to find another use for his yards and yards of brown denim canvas. The first generation of jeans was born. They were christened "waist overalls."

Then the second chance event occurred. Jacob Davis, a Nevada tailor who frequently bought bolts of cloth at Levi Strauss & Co., invented a method of strengthening the trousers. He placed metal rivets at pocket corners and at the base of the fly. He did not have the money to apply for a patent for his idea, so he sent Levi a letter. Perhaps Mr. Strauss would be interested in

GO ON

READING: COMPREHENSION

● Lesson 11: Nonfiction (cont.)

paying for the paperwork so that the two men could apply for the patent together. Strauss agreed. Rivets were added to the stress points of Levi's denim waist overalls, and the second generation of jeans was born. The term *jeans* was born out of the name of an Italian city, Genoa, where denim could be purchased.

Jeans did not change the life of Mr. Strauss significantly. He and Jacob Davis did earn good money from their successful riveted denim trousers, but Mr. Strauss was already a wealthy man. Denim jeans did significantly alter the lives for the rest of us. The Levi Strauss Company boasts that jeans are the only garment invented in the nineteenth century that are still worn today.

1. **The main idea of this reading is—**
   - (A) the California Gold Rush.
   - (B) the creation of the world's first pair of jeans.
   - (C) panning for gold in California.
   - (D) holding court in the Early West.

2. **The first chance occurrence in the creation of jeans was—**
   - (F) the lack of clothing by the miners.
   - (G) the interest of Jacob Davis in using rivets to strengthen the jeans.
   - (H) the mild weather in California which ruled out the market for denim.
   - (J) the building Strauss bought in San Francisco.

3. **Which offers the best conclusion to this success story?**
   - (A) Levi Strauss was fortunate to have been where he was when he was.
   - (B) Strauss was wealthy prior to creating his denim jeans.
   - (C) Conestoga wagons helped bring miners to California.
   - (D) Jacob Davis was very jealous of the success of Strauss.

4. **Which is not a fact?**
   - (F) Strauss was a Bavarian immigrant.
   - (G) The first jeans of Strauss were called "waist overalls."
   - (H) Both Levi Strauss and Jacob Davis applied for the patent.
   - (J) Strauss was fortunate to have a friend like Jacob Davis.

5. **The setting for this passage is—**
   - (A) Bavaria.
   - (B) Southern California.
   - (C) San Francisco area.
   - (D) New York City.

6. **The time setting for this passage could best be described as—**
   - (F) the early 1900s.
   - (G) the 1850s.
   - (H) the 1700s.
   - (J) the 1820s.

STOP

READING: COMPREHENSION

● **Lesson 12: Nonfiction**

Directions: Read each item carefully. Then choose the correct answer and fill in the circle that corresponds to that choice.

Example

Freezing retards the growth of molds, yeasts, bacteria, and enzymes in foods. However it is not the only method of preserving perishables. Dehydrating, canning, pickling, and applying chemical additives are additional methods of preserving the freshness, appearance, and nutritional value of foods.

A. **Which of the following best defines the underlined word in the passage to the left?**

(A) foods likely to spoil

(B) freeze-dried foods

(C) frozen foods

(D) pickled foods

Clue

Skim the passage and then answer the questions. Refer back to the passage to find the answers. You don't have to reread the passage for each question.

● **Practice**

Matthew Brady's Plan to End Warfare

Matthew Brady opened his first photography studio in 1844. The images produced were daguerreotypes, recorded images on sheets of copper coated with silver. They required long exposures to produce the image. A person being photographed would have to stay perfectly still for three to fifteen minutes. That made daguerreotypes impractical for portraits. By 1855, though, Brady was advertising a new type of image that had just been invented: a photograph made on paper.

From the beginning of his career, Brady thought that photography could serve an important purpose. His images could create a record of national life. When the Civil War broke out, he wanted to document the war. Although his costs were prohibitive and his friends discouraged him, he assembled a corps of photographers. He also bought photographs from others returning from the field. His efforts culminated in an 1862 display of photographs made after the Battle of Antietam. The bloodshed shocked the exhibit's visitors, most of whom had never known what warfare was like.

His goal was to use powerful photos to end all war. Brady did not stop warfare, of course. He did not even earn enough money to pay for his venture. After the Civil War, people lost interest in his chronicle of the war. He found few buyers for the photographs. He went bankrupt. Years after the war, Congress bought his collection, but he earned only enough money to pay the debts that had built up while he assembled the collection.

Still, Brady recorded one of the most important episodes in American history. In doing so, he created the first photo-documentation of a war.

GO ON

READING: COMPREHENSION

● Lesson 12: Nonfiction (cont.)

1. **The main idea of this passage is—**
   - Ⓐ Matthew Brady's photographs.
   - Ⓑ the Civil War.
   - Ⓒ the plan of Matthew Brady to end warfare.
   - Ⓓ portrait photography in the 1800s.

2. **The new technology that helped Brady to photograph real life was—**
   - Ⓕ the daguerreotype.
   - Ⓖ photographs made on paper.
   - Ⓗ digital images.
   - Ⓙ photosynthesis.

3. **Which of these occupations would best describe Matthew Brady's work?**
   - Ⓐ combat soldier
   - Ⓑ portrait photographer
   - Ⓒ photojournalist
   - Ⓓ wedding photographer

4. **Matthew Brady went bankrupt because—**
   - Ⓕ his photographs weren't very good.
   - Ⓖ there were few buyers for his photographs.
   - Ⓗ other photographers had already done the same thing.
   - Ⓙ he was never paid by Congress.

5. **The time setting for this passage on Matthew Brady was—**
   - Ⓐ the 1500s.
   - Ⓑ the 1600s.
   - Ⓒ the 1700s.
   - Ⓓ the 1800s.

6. **Brady wanted his photos to—**
   - Ⓕ create a record of national life.
   - Ⓖ create a pathway for young photographers.
   - Ⓗ develop a school for Hudson River photography.
   - Ⓙ set a standard for excellence in portrait photography.

7. **Daguerreotypes are images recorded on—**
   - Ⓐ typing paper.
   - Ⓑ copper sheets.
   - Ⓒ silver nitrate.
   - Ⓓ plaster.

READING: COMPREHENSION

● Lesson 13: Fiction

Directions: Read each item carefully. Then choose the correct answer and fill in the circle that corresponds to that choice.

Example

The museum was a treat for my senses. The paintings had colors that tickled my eyes. I enjoyed listening to the guide's happy voice when she talked about the artists. And even though we weren't allowed to touch anything, I could feel the pictures in my mind. The guide told us that some artists mainly like to paint nature while others prefer painting people or interesting designs.

A. **The author in this story is telling us about—**

Ⓐ museums.

Ⓑ fire safety at the museum.

Ⓒ the enjoyment experienced during a visit to an art museum.

Ⓓ the colors that appeal to the senses.

Clue

Skim the passage and then answer the questions. Refer back to the passage to find the answers. You don't have to reread the passage for each question.

● Practice

They Had It So Good!

"Eighth grade is just killing me!" complained Bo. "There's one test after another, teachers yelling, pressure from parents to get good grades. You'd think we were seniors in high school. I mean, we have four more years after this one! Maybe I don't even want to go to college.

"We're living in the wrong time. I wish we lived in the 1800s. Kids didn't go to school much, especially those who lived on farms."

Emily came over. "I couldn't help hearing," she said. "And, far be it for me to burst your little bubble, but I wouldn't want to be a pioneer." Everybody sort of rolled their eyes. Miss Know-it-all was about to impart her wisdom again.

Emily continued. "Pioneer families left their homes to travel in Conestoga wagons that would leak or break down. They would be attacked by Native Americans who didn't want more settlers taking their land. Horses would die, guides would desert them, there were bandits on the road, and chances were that even if they got where they were going, the land would be a big disappointment.

"The land might be rocky and not even worth farming. If the pioneers saw that the Native Americans were going to stay, they often just burned them out. Nobody ever asked the Native Americans permission to use their land, much less own it! Kids worked from sunup to sundown on these farms. Food might be scarce, so often all they'd get at dinner

GO ON

READING: COMPREHENSION

● Lesson 13: Fiction (cont.)

would be some watery stew or potatoes. Water was usually far from the house, so most people only bathed once a week if they were lucky.

"Doesn't sound so good, huh? Some places had no trees, so forget the cozy log house. A room dug into a hillside with sod for a roof might be the best you could do. And, you'd be so lonely for other people, you'd welcome school. Of course every grade would be taught in a one-room schoolhouse. There'd be no paper, just little blackboards. You might have to walk miles in the snow, and…"

Bo stood up and began to leave! "Enough!" he said. "Any more of this, and you'll have me being happy about school." Emily smiled. Another mission accomplished, she thought.

1. **The main idea of this passage is—**
    - (A) Bo's distaste for school.
    - (B) difficult times in pioneer days.
    - (C) kids only went to school when chores were done.
    - (D) Bo wanted to run away from home.

2. **All were disadvantages of going to school in pioneer days except—**
    - (F) the possibility of Indian attacks.
    - (G) travel to and from school was dangerous.
    - (H) the land was poor as were most of the people.
    - (J) there would not have been the pressure associated with today's expectations in school.

3. **After listening to Emily, Bo probably came to this conclusion.**
    - (A) Going to school today is a much better experience than it was in the 1800s.
    - (B) Pioneer children had it made.
    - (C) People didn't care much about their health in the 1800s.
    - (D) Kids today work much harder than children of the 1800s.

4. **Which is not a fact?**
    - (F) Emily's views on going to school were much better than Bo's.
    - (G) Children during the 1800s didn't go to school for as long as children today.
    - (H) Pioneers faced many dangers during the 1800s.
    - (J) There is more pressure on children to succeed in today's schools.

5. **The main characters are—**
    - (A) the pioneers and the Indians.
    - (B) school children during the 1800s.
    - (C) Bo and Emily.
    - (D) parents and teachers.

6. **What grade are these students in?**
    - (F) seventh
    - (G) eighth
    - (H) ninth

7. **The early pioneers traveled west in—**
    - (A) Conestoga wagons.
    - (B) family cars.
    - (C) horse-drawn carriages.
    - (D) mule-drawn carts.

STOP

Name _____   Date_____

━━━━━━ *READING: COMPREHENSION* ━━━━━━

● **Lesson 14: Fiction**

Directions: Read each item carefully. Then choose the correct answer and fill in the circle that corresponds to that choice.

Example

Courtney needed a summer job, so she responded to an ad in the local newspaper for someone to stock shelves. Courtney was pleased when she was called in for an interview. On her way to the interview, she wondered what she would be stocking on those shelves. She was delighted to find out that it was a music store as CDs were among her favorite things.

A. What is a fact from the passage?

- Ⓐ Courtney liked country music as much as anyone.
- Ⓑ Courtney was granted an interview for the job.
- Ⓒ Stocking CDs is much better work than stocking DVDs.
- Ⓓ Anyone can get a job from a newspaper ad.

Clue Skim the passage. Then answer the questions. Refer back to the passage to find the answers. You don't have to reread the passage for each question.

● **Practice**

One Step at a Time

Tracy studied the girls ahead of her, numbers pinned to each hunter-green shirt. Tracy's was kelly green. She bit her lip. "Don't worry about everything all at once," her grandmother always told her. "Break each problem into little steps."

How? No way was she going to be able to smile. Her back tucks had been so low yesterday that she'd landed on her knees. She'd been chanting too fast all week. One step at a time, she told herself, but her chest tightened.

The gym door opened, and a girl slipped inside. Tracy heard a faint "Go, Eagles!" What if she started before the judges gave her the signal? She shook her head. Worry about the tumbling. Impossible to break even that into separate steps. She had to get her timing

right, keep her feet together, remember not to make duck hands. She moaned, stepping out of line.

"Where are you going?" the girl behind her said. "You're next."

Next? The gym door opened. The girl pushed Tracy inside. The judges sat at a table all the way across the polished gym floor. Tracy swallowed. She was going to throw up. She was going to faint. All those faces watching. All that distance to go.

She let her breath out in a long hiss, then took off. Halfway into her hurdle, she remembered that she hadn't yelled, hadn't made any hand signals. She pitched forward, then caught herself. Her heart thundered, and she couldn't move. Just go forward, she

GO ON

Published by Spectrum. Copyright protected.   **30**   1-57768-978-X *Spectrum Test Practice 8*

READING: COMPREHENSION

● Lesson 14: Fiction (cont.)

told herself. Just take the first step. On the second flip-flop, she realized she was rebounding high enough. She hurled herself through the back tuck, landing on both feet. She grinned, yelled "Go, Eagles," then ran forward. One step at a time.

1. What is the main idea in the passage?

Ⓐ Tracy's self esteem

Ⓑ Tracy trying to remember her routine

Ⓒ The advice of Tracy's grandmother for solving problems

Ⓓ Tracy becomes a cheerleader for the Eagles

2. Tracy's first worry was—

Ⓕ to land on her feet.

Ⓖ to cheer for the Eagles.

Ⓗ to make a graceful flip in the middle of the routine.

Ⓙ the tumbling.

3. Once Tracy completes her tumbling routine and shouts, "Go, Eagles," we think—

Ⓐ she is going to become a cheerleader.

Ⓑ she still lacks in self-esteem.

Ⓒ she needs to try harder.

Ⓓ she needs to get another hobby.

4. Which is an opinion?

Ⓕ The judges sat across the gym floor.

Ⓖ Tracy was very nervous about her tryout.

Ⓗ Tracy had a number pinned to her green shirt.

Ⓙ Her grandmother had some very sound advice for solving problems.

5. The main character in this passage is—

Ⓐ Tracy's grandmother.

Ⓑ Tracy's sister.

Ⓒ Tracy.

Ⓓ the judges.

6. What color was Tracy's shirt?

Ⓕ red

Ⓖ blue

Ⓗ gold

Ⓙ green

7. What was the school's nickname?

Ⓐ Wildcats

Ⓑ Hoosiers

Ⓒ Rams

Ⓓ Eagles

━━━━━━━━━━ **READING: COMPREHENSION** ━━━━━━━━━━

● **Lesson 15: Fiction**

Directions: Read each item carefully. Then choose the correct answer and fill in the circle that corresponds to that choice.

┌─────────── **Example** ───────────┐

I have just finished my trip down the Congo River and am applying for entrance to your club. I have the $1,000 entry fee and am including the tale and photographs of an amazing adventure. This tale demonstrates my ability to face challenges. I hope you accept me.

A. **What is the goal of the person who wrote this letter?**

Ⓐ to travel the entire length of the Congo River

Ⓑ to become a member of the Congo Club

Ⓒ to win the $1,000 prize for best entry

Ⓓ to see the Congo River from a helicopter

Clue Skim the passage and then answer the questions. Refer back to the passage to find the answers. You don't have to reread the passage for each question.

● **Practice**

Letter to the Governor

Dear Governor,

I am a 12-year-old Native American who is in the seventh grade. I grew up on a reservation, but this year my family moved to Tucson because my mom thinks the schools here are better for me. I miss my home a lot. One thing I really miss is being able to drive.

I am writing to you because I think the minimum age for getting a driver's license in our state is way too high. Why do we have to be 16 before we can get a license? We can't even get a driver's permit until we are 15 1/2. It is unfair because kids are just as able to drive as adults. They just need the chance to learn.

I know this because I know how to drive. So do my friends on the reservation. We practiced in the fields and on the back roads, and now we are all good drivers. If I had a driver's license, I could get around more easily because I would not need to beg others for rides. Please consider lowering the minimum age for getting a driver's license.

Sincerely yours,

Maria Miguel

GO ON

READING: COMPREHENSION

● Lesson 15: Fiction (cont.)

1. **Which is the main idea of this letter to the governor?**
   - (A) to drive a car the entire length of the state of Arizona
   - (B) to obtain a driver's license to drive around the reservation
   - (C) to get a driver's license at the age of 12
   - (D) to lower the age for getting a driver's license to 15

2. **Which expresses the feelings of the writer?**
   - (F) She feels the age of getting a driver's license is unfair.
   - (G) She doesn't want to live on the reservation any more.
   - (H) She doesn't want to go to school in Tucson.
   - (J) She prefers driving a Jeep to a Honda.

3. **Why do you think the young Native American wants her license?**
   - (A) She wants to show other children how well she can drive a car.
   - (B) She thinks she can drive as well as adults because of her experience.
   - (C) She wants a new car.
   - (D) She prefers driving to school to wearing a pair of roller skates.

4. **Which is a fact?**
   - (F) Native Americans are the best drivers.
   - (G) The earlier you learn to drive, the better driver you become.
   - (H) Young children are better drivers than adults.
   - (J) This 12-year old was allowed to drive on the reservation.

5. **The main character in this passage is—**
   - (A) a Native American.
   - (B) a California drifter.
   - (C) a parent from Illinois.
   - (D) an auto mechanic.

6. **What city does this young girl now call home?**
   - (F) New York City
   - (G) Cleveland
   - (H) Los Angeles
   - (J) Tucson

7. **Where did she learn how to drive?**
   - (A) driver's education program at school
   - (B) from a private driver education program
   - (C) on a reservation
   - (D) in Tucson, Arizona

STOP

Name _____ Date _____

● **Directions:** Read each item carefully. Then choose the correct answer and fill in the circle that corresponds to that choice.

Example

She had never been inside a mine shaft. She had no friends or relatives who worked as coal miners. The old dressmaker, who frequently wore a shawl and a bonnet, seemed a highly unlikely candidate for the position of motivator for the mine workers.

A. **Which of the following is a fact?**
- Ⓐ Women make better miners than men.
- Ⓑ Coal mining is a very dangerous business.
- Ⓒ Women should not be allowed to wear a bonnet into the mine.
- Ⓓ The woman in this passage had never been in a mine shaft.

Skim the passage and then answer the questions. Refer back to the passage to find the answers. You don't have to reread the passage for each question.

E-mail Alert

U.S. Representative David McDavid today introduced Bill 409 to the House of Representatives. McDavid reports that Internet e-mail and instant messaging services cost the U.S. Postal Service in lost postage fees. Bill 409 would permit the U.S. Postal Service to charge a five-cent surcharge on each e-mail sent. The U.S. Postal Service would bill the Internet service provider, which would in turn charge the sender of the e-mail. Representative McDavid reports that no final decision has been made on charging for instant messaging services. This surcharge may be added to the bill at a later time. Attorney Ronald Sneed of Omaha, Nebraska, has agreed to fight this bill, filing a class-action suit on behalf of a group of frequent Internet users. Sneed has asked that citizens forward this e-mail to everyone on their mailing list, in order to alert citizens of this new charge.

1. **According to this alert, David McDavid is—**
- Ⓐ a U.S. Congressman.
- Ⓑ a U.S. Senator.
- Ⓒ an interested citizen.
- Ⓓ the Director of Consumer Affairs.

2. **The main concern of this article is—**
- Ⓕ the role of Congress.
- Ⓖ undocumented claims.
- Ⓗ possible charges imposed by the U.S. Postal Service for e-mail messages.
- Ⓙ there is no concern expressed in this article.

GO ON

The Underwater Jungle

Can you imagine a wilderness under the sea that is so humongous it has never been fully explored? The Great Barrier Reef is such a place, being the largest ridge of coral in the world. It is 1,250 miles long—that's about as far as the distance between Detroit, Michigan, and Houston, Texas. Its undersea coral gardens provide homes for more than 1,400 varieties of exotic fish. This huge maritime province stretches along the northeastern coast of Australia and ranges from 10 to more than 100 miles from the shore.

In 1770, English explorer Captain James Cook discovered the reef on his way to Antarctica. His ship was the first of many to be damaged on the treacherous, sharp coral lying just below the ocean's surface. In fact, the reef is a graveyard to more than 500 ships. Navigational charts are marked in some places with the warning "Unexamined but considered dangerous to navigation." The weather causes other hazards to ships. Sometimes whole islands disappear in great storms called cyclones which change reef maps overnight.

Danger also lies down in the reef. Huge awesome creatures lurk in its crevices. Sea snakes with venom in their fangs swim with 10-foot moray eels. Sea crocodiles, sea turtles, giant clams, and 600-pound groper fish with a mythic reputation for eating people also reside among the coral. And, if that's not enough, manta rays, weighing four tons and having a wing span of 20 feet, keep company with 35-foot, extremely dangerous, white sharks. One resident, the 70-foot whale shark, is friendly. His diet consists of anchovies, without the pizza!

The reef is made up mainly of little animals called coral polyps, which are one-half inch or less long. Their colonies resemble multicolored flowers and vegetables. The greatest enemy of the polyps is the crown of thorns starfish. Named for the venomous spines of their bodies, these starfish are enormous eaters, and their favorite fast-food restaurant is the Great Barrier Reef. One starfish can strip the polyps from seven square feet of coral a week, leaving a wasteland behind. They are sometimes 24 inches in width with up to 23 arms. When they are chopped up, they regenerate. If an arm is cut off, it grows back! It's no wonder you can see up to 5,000 starfish in one small area! This starfish invasion is quite recent, large numbers having started to appear in the 1960s. One theory to explain this population explosion is that man-made pollution has somehow given starfish a survival edge over conditions that previously held their numbers down. But if humans try to radically interfere and stop the starfish, the situation could be made even worse. Interfering with nature often yields awful results.

This sea garden has problems other than starfish. Oil rigs, mining, wrecked ships, and tourists also harm the reef. Commercial interests, wishing to develop and mine the area, often grab up pieces as fast as the starfish.

GO ON

The Australian government is working hard to keep the reef structures intact. The Great Barrier Reef Marine Park Authority has sea and air rangers. They believe the ecological balance must be preserved. Maybe one day you will be able to visit the reef.

3. **What is the topic of the reading selection "The Underwater Jungle"?**
   - (A) sea creatures
   - (B) the Great Barrier Reef
   - (C) wrecked ships
   - (D) starfish

4. **What is the main idea of the second paragraph?**
   - (F) The sharp coral and the weather cause hazards for ships.
   - (G) Captain Cook discovered the Great Barrier Reef.
   - (H) The Reef is a graveyard to 500 wrecked ships.
   - (J) Sometimes cyclones cause whole islands to disappear.

5. **In paragraph three, which statement(s) support(s) the paragraph's main idea, "Danger also lies down in the Reef"?**
   - (A) Sea snakes and moray eels live in the crevices.
   - (B) Manta rays and white sharks are found in the reef.
   - (C) Sea crocodiles, sea turtles, giant clams, and groper fish are residents.
   - (D) All of these choices.

6. **What is the main idea of paragraph four?**
   - (F) If a starfish loses an arm, it grows another.
   - (G) The crown of thorns starfish are destroying the reef.
   - (H) The reef is made up of coral polyps.
   - (J) Man-made pollution has helped the starfish population to explode.

7. **Which of these statements is not true?**
   - (A) The Great Barrier Reef Marine Park Authority has sea and air rangers.
   - (B) Captain James Cook discovered the Great Barrier Reef on his way to the Arctic.
   - (C) The Great Barrier Reef is 1,250 miles long.
   - (D) Crown of thorns starfish are sometimes two feet wide.

8. **Which is not a danger to the Great Barrier Reef?**
   - (F) crown of thorns starfish
   - (G) tourists
   - (H) oil rigs
   - (J) ecologists

9. **Which of these inhabitants of the Great Barrier Reef does not pose a danger to humans?**
   - (A) whale shark
   - (B) white shark
   - (C) sea crocodiles
   - (D) manta rays

GO ON

Name _____ Date_____

Great Faces in High Places

If you were driving in the Black Hills of South Dakota about 25 miles southwest of Rapid City and saw four faces on a mountain looking at you, you would not be seeing things! You would be viewing Mt. Rushmore, a national memorial with the images of four American Presidents carved in the mountain's granite.

The 60-foot heads of Presidents George Washington, Thomas Jefferson, Theodore Roosevelt, and Abraham Lincoln were chiseled in the 6,000-foot-high mountain by American sculptor Gutzon Borglum. He began his task in August of 1927 primarily using dynamite and a jackhammer to alter the mountain side.

He completed his first figure, Washington, for a dedication on July 4, 1930. Borglum died in 1941, but his son Lincoln was able to continue the work. Their studio still exists showcasing the Borglums' scale models, bits, chisels, hammers, and other tools.

It took 14 years to carve the faces on Mt. Rushmore, although only six and one-half were spent in actual work by the father and son. The job was held up by bad weather and lack of funds. The total cost was just under one million dollars, of which the federal government paid approximately 84%. Private donations made up the rest of the amount.

Over 2,000,000 people visit Mt. Rushmore each year to see the memorial that was first suggested in 1923 by Jonah Robinson of the South Dakota State Historical Society. The idea was approved, and the mountain was established as a national memorial in 1925.

The mountain was named after a New York lawyer, Charles E. Rushmore, who visited the area in 1885. Traveling through the area, he asked a prospector the name of the mountain and since it had no name, the prospector looked at the lawyer and said with a grin, "Rushmore." The name stuck.

Each of the heads on the mountain represent an aspect of the United States. Borglum selected George Washington to represent the founding of the nation, since he was the first President. Thomas Jefferson, the country's third President, wrote the Declaration of Independence and represents the nation's political philosophy. Abraham Lincoln, the 16th President, represents preservation of the nation. He was elected in 1861 and served during the United States' Civil War. He refused to let the nation be divided and brought about the emancipation of the slaves in the South. Theodore Roosevelt represents the expansion and conservation of the nation. After becoming the 26th President, his administration set aside 194,000,000 additional acres of land for parks and saved mineral, oil, coal, and waterpower sites for future generations.

Mount Rushmore, a marvel of artistic and engineering skill, demonstrates a belief Gutzon Borglum held: "A monument's dimensions should be determined by the importance to civilization of the events commemorated." The gigantic sculpture is awe-inspiring.

READING: COMPREHENSION
SAMPLE TEST (cont.)

10. **What is the main idea of the selection?**
    - (F) man's dominance over nature
    - (G) a boost to South Dakota tourism
    - (H) a memorial to four great American presidents
    - (J) private donations for the public good

11. **Which of these American presidents is not etched in stone on Mt. Rushmore?**
    - (A) John F. Kennedy
    - (B) Abraham Lincoln
    - (C) Theodore Roosevelt
    - (D) George Washington

12. **Who was the sculptor of this great monument?**
    - (F) Claude Monet
    - (G) Gutzon Borglum
    - (H) Jonah Robinson
    - (J) Robinson William Caruso

13. **Which description is incorrect?**
    - (A) George Washington represents the founding of the nation.
    - (B) Abraham Lincoln represents the preservation of the nation.
    - (C) Theodore Roosevelt represents the expansion of the nation.
    - (D) Thomas Jefferson represents the poetry of the nation.

14. **The location of this great monument is—**
    - (F) near Kansas City, Missouri.
    - (G) near Rapid City, South Dakota.
    - (H) near Billings, Montana.
    - (J) near Cheyenne, Wyoming.

15. **Who among the following was the second sculptor to work on the monument?**
    - (A) Chandler Westinghouse
    - (B) Evan Fitzsimmons
    - (C) Lincoln Borglum
    - (D) Charles E. Rushmore

16. **How long did it take to complete the memorial from start to finish?**
    - (F) a full year
    - (G) three years
    - (H) ten years
    - (J) fourteen years

ANSWER SHEET

STUDENT'S NAME

LAST	FIRST	MI

SCHOOL

TEACHER

FEMALE ○   MALE ○

BIRTH DATE

MONTH	DAY	YEAR

MONTH: JAN ○ FEB ○ MAR ○ APR ○ MAY ○ JUN ○ JUL ○ AUG ○ SEP ○ OCT ○ NOV ○ DEC ○

DAY: (0)(1)(2)(3) (0)(1)(2)(3)(4)(5)(6)(7)(8)(9)

YEAR: (0)(1)(2)(3)(4)(5)(6)(7)(8)(9) (5)(6)(7)(8)(9)(0)

GRADE
(7) (8) (9)

(Student name grid columns each with letters A through Z)

Part 1: VOCABULARY

A	(A)(B)(C)(D)
B	(F)(G)(H)(J)
1	(A)(B)(C)(D)
2	(F)(G)(H)(J)
3	(A)(B)(C)(D)
4	(F)(G)(H)(J)

5	(A)(B)(C)(D)
6	(F)(G)(H)(J)
7	(A)(B)(C)(D)
8	(F)(G)(H)(J)
9	(A)(B)(C)(D)
10	(F)(G)(H)(J)

11	(A)(B)(C)(D)
12	(F)(G)(H)(J)
13	(A)(B)(C)(D)
14	(F)(G)(H)(J)
15	(A)(B)(C)(D)
16	(F)(G)(H)(J)

17	(A)(B)(C)(D)
18	(F)(G)(H)(J)
19	(A)(B)(C)(D)
20	(F)(G)(H)(J)
21	(A)(B)(C)(D)
22	(F)(G)(H)(J)

23	(A)(B)(C)(D)
24	(F)(G)(H)(J)
25	(A)(B)(C)(D)
26	(F)(G)(H)(J)
27	(A)(B)(C)(D)
28	(F)(G)(H)(J)

29	(A)(B)(C)(D)
30	(F)(G)(H)(J)
31	(A)(B)(C)(D)
32	(F)(G)(H)(J)

Part 2: COMPREHENSION

A	(A)(B)(C)(D)
1	(A)(B)(C)(D)
2	(F)(G)(H)(J)
3	(A)(B)(C)(D)

4	(F)(G)(H)(J)
5	(A)(B)(C)(D)
6	(F)(G)(H)(J)
7	(A)(B)(C)(D)

8	(F)(G)(H)(J)
9	(A)(B)(C)(D)
10	(F)(G)(H)(J)
11	(A)(B)(C)(D)

12	(F)(G)(H)(J)
13	(A)(B)(C)(D)
14	(F)(G)(H)(J)

1-57768-978-X Spectrum Test Practice 8

READING PRACTICE TEST

● Part 1: Vocabulary

Directions: For Example A, find the word that means the same as the underlined word. For Example B, find the word that means the opposite of the underlined word.

Examples

A.   gruesome costume

- Ⓐ beautiful
- Ⓑ exquisite
- Ⓒ ghastly
- Ⓓ sublime

B.   forthright opinion

- Ⓕ stealthy
- Ⓖ sincere
- Ⓗ honest
- Ⓙ genuine

For numbers 1–8, read each item. Choose the answer that means the same or about the same as the underlined word.

1. **gorgeous actress**
   - Ⓐ homely
   - Ⓑ talented
   - Ⓒ beautiful
   - Ⓓ dedicated

2. **an immaculate bedroom**
   - Ⓕ jumbled
   - Ⓖ unkempt
   - Ⓗ tidy
   - Ⓙ cluttered

3. **contribute to the charity**
   - Ⓐ donate
   - Ⓑ scramble
   - Ⓒ reimburse
   - Ⓓ work

4. **demolish the house**
   - Ⓕ build
   - Ⓖ destroy
   - Ⓗ construct
   - Ⓙ remodel

5. **exit the state**
   - Ⓐ commence
   - Ⓑ stand
   - Ⓒ enter
   - Ⓓ leave

6. **desolate land**
   - Ⓕ lonely
   - Ⓖ cozy
   - Ⓗ fertile
   - Ⓙ difficult

7. **intelligent student**
   - Ⓐ tardy
   - Ⓑ smart
   - Ⓒ punctual
   - Ⓓ hungry

8. **unbiased jury**
   - Ⓕ relaxed
   - Ⓖ impartial
   - Ⓗ lonely
   - Ⓙ prejudiced

GO ON

READING PRACTICE TEST
Part 1: Vocabulary (cont.)

For numbers 9–16, read each item. Choose the answer that is the opposite of the underlined word.

9. **punctual** student
   - (A) foolish
   - (B) average
   - (C) intelligent
   - (D) tardy

10. **impoverished** college student
    - (F) wealthy
    - (G) poor
    - (H) grateful
    - (J) clumsy

11. loud **moan**
    - (A) laugh
    - (B) wail
    - (C) shout
    - (D) movement

12. **dishonest** response
    - (F) hostile
    - (G) candid
    - (H) raucous
    - (J) edited

13. **talkative**
    - (A) gabby
    - (B) garrulous
    - (C) chatty
    - (D) mute

14. **merge** the documents
    - (F) separate
    - (G) bring together
    - (H) cast aside
    - (J) edit

15. a **famine**
    - (A) drought
    - (B) time of plenty
    - (C) escape
    - (D) dedication

16. **irrelevant**
    - (F) unnecessary
    - (G) unimportant
    - (H) nonessential
    - (J) important

GO ON

READING PRACTICE TEST
Part 1: Vocabulary (cont.)

For numbers 17–20, choose the word that best completes each sentence.

17. Mei and I _____ to spend the summer backpacking across Europe.
    - (A) revolved
    - (B) resolved
    - (C) fluctuated
    - (D) remembered

18. We slept in hostels and cooked our meals in _____ kitchens.
    - (F) capricious
    - (G) coexist
    - (H) communal
    - (J) company

19. Mei's guidebook had _____ descriptions of famous attractions.
    - (A) succinct
    - (B) compatible
    - (C) blatant
    - (D) curt

20. We got lost, arriving at Blackheath Castle by a _____ route.
    - (F) direct
    - (G) linear
    - (H) picturesque
    - (J) roundabout

For numbers 21–24, read each item. Choose the word that correctly completes both sentences.

21. We set up our camp near the _____ of the mountain.
    The runner rounded first _____ and headed for second.
    - (A) foot
    - (B) base
    - (C) home
    - (D) crest

22. We can only _____ corn when the field dries out.
    We visited a bottling _____.
    - (F) harvest
    - (G) pick
    - (H) factory
    - (J) plant

23. The teacher asked her students to openly _____ their opinions.
    The Deerfield Zepher is an _____ commuter that makes only one stop.
    - (A) express
    - (B) fast
    - (C) shout
    - (D) open

24. Tami couldn't clean the _____ in the collar of her shirt.
    You can win a prize if you can _____ the bell.
    - (F) dirt
    - (G) ring
    - (H) shoot
    - (J) capture

GO ON

READING PRACTICE TEST
Part 1: Vocabulary (cont.)

For numbers 25–32, read the paragraph. Find the word below the paragraph that fits best in each numbered blank.

To travel across the desert, there is one **(25)**_____ rule. Make your trip with water! The desert is not always flat. There are sometimes **(26)**_____. Because the desert is so dry, the plants do not **(27)**_____ many flowers. The climate of the desert is dry and never **(28)**_____. A footprint in the desert would quickly **(29)**_____ in the blowing sand. There's not just one kind of cactus, but **(30)**_____ species of cactuses living in the desert. Wearing sunglasses is a good **(31)**_____ if you are in the desert sun. The desert sun is very **(32)**_____.

25.
- (A) absolute
- (B) nearly
- (C) unknown
- (D) untested

26.
- (F) problems
- (G) transients
- (H) tables
- (J) dunes

27.
- (A) handle
- (B) harvest
- (C) bear
- (D) clip

28.
- (F) arid
- (G) hot
- (H) muggy
- (J) protected

29.
- (A) appear
- (B) vast
- (C) compare
- (D) vanish

30.
- (F) singular
- (G) diverse
- (H) absolute
- (J) twelve

31.
- (A) map
- (B) precaution
- (C) complete
- (D) condition

32.
- (F) dry
- (G) insulated
- (H) intense
- (J) common

STOP

READING PRACTICE TEST

● Part 2: Comprehension

Directions: Read each article in this section carefully. Then choose the correct answer and fill in the circle that corresponds to that choice.

Example

Do you know how television works? The picture taken by the camera is turned into an electronic pulse that is broadcast into the air. The receiver in your television picks up the signal and turns it into the picture you see on the screen.

A. **In this passage, the word *broadcast* means**
- (A) received
- (B) sent
- (C) created
- (D) weakened

Giant of the Forest

Every part of the country has a special tree that is native to that region. On the northwest coast of the United States, that special tree is called the redwood. These tall, reddish-brown trees grow in beautiful forests, usually near the ocean. Redwood trees need a great deal of moisture, and being near the ocean provides them with ample exposure to rain and fog.

Redwoods grow to be very old, with some living for hundreds of years. Scientists know the age of any of these trees by looking at its growth rings. If a redwood tree is cut crossways, you can see these rings. A ring is formed for each year of a tree's life. Researchers study redwood tree rings not only to learn the age of the tree, but to learn what the climate and environmental conditions were like in the forest as the tree was growing.

Redwood trees are ecologically important. Most of them are protected in state and national parks and won't be cut for lumber.

Redwoods exist in ecosystems that depend on trees for survival. The branches and leaves of redwoods collect moisture that feeds the tree and sustains the forest life below it. Many different species of flowers, plants, insects, and vertebrate animals coexist with redwoods. It is not uncommon to see deer, birds, slugs, ferns, and flowers when walking through a dense redwood forest.

Unlike most other trees, redwoods are fairly resistant to insects and floods. Redwood trees are also fire-resistant to some extent, and even depend on periodic, low-intensity fires to clear away ground cover and encourage new growth. Most redwoods that die naturally die from being knocked over by high winds.

Even after a redwood tree falls, it has an important role to play in the forest. It can take hundreds of years for a dead redwood log to decompose completely. During that time, the log is home to many animals and various types of fungus. The impact these creatures have on the log helps it to break down and become part of the soil where seeds will start new life.

GO ON

READING: PRACTICE TEST
Part 2: Comprehension (cont.)

1. **This article is mostly about—**
   - (A) how a forest grows.
   - (B) how to identify forest plants.
   - (C) forest animals and birds.
   - (D) a unique kind of tree.

2. **The author says that many animals and plants "coexist with redwoods." The word** *coexist* **probably means—**
   - (F) compete for food.
   - (G) struggle for life.
   - (H) live together.
   - (J) have common enemies.

3. **Low-intensity forest fires help redwood forests because—**
   - (A) they scare away animals and birds.
   - (B) the old undergrowth is burned away.
   - (C) they help the trees to decompose faster.
   - (D) they turn the tree bark a reddish color.

4. **Choose the sentence that best supports your answer for number 2.**
   - (F) A forest always includes animals and plants.
   - (G) Without animals, there wouldn't be any trees.
   - (H) There is competition between animals and plants.
   - (J) The forest is an extremely wild place.

5. **Select the sentence that best summarizes the life cycle of a redwood tree.**
   - (A) When a redwood tree dies, the log is always made into lumber.
   - (B) Redwoods grow, die, and decompose all within one year.
   - (C) A redwood tree dies only when it is knocked over by the wind.
   - (D) Redwood trees grow, die, then decompose into the earth.

6. **Which of these facts about the passage helps identify it as a** *descriptive passage*?
   - (F) It is written in question-and-answer format.
   - (G) It gives steps and teaches a new technique.
   - (H) It includes a wide range of information.
   - (J) It is about something that is found in nature.

7. **If you wanted to find out more about redwood trees, which of these resources would be most helpful?**
   - (A) an encyclopedia
   - (B) a college dictionary
   - (C) a world atlas
   - (D) a United States map

GO ON

READING: PRACTICE TEST
Part 2: Comprehension (cont.)

Read carefully. Answer the items on page 47.

A New Favorite Pastime

Baseball is often referred to as America's favorite pastime. Collecting baseball cards is another favorite pastime of Americans, young and old. It's a fun hobby, and for some lucky people it has become a good investment. Baseball cards can be worth a lot of money. Finding a special one can be like discovering buried treasure. For instance, if you found a baseball card with a picture of Honus Wagner of the Pittsburgh Pirates, you would have a card worth as much as $400,000! In 1936, he was one of the first five players inducted into the Baseball Hall of Fame in Cooperstown, New York.

However, not all cards are worth a lot of money. You can buy a card for as little as a penny. Wouldn't it be fun to buy a rookie card for a penny and then sell it ten years later for $10? A "rookie" is a beginning player in either the National or American Leagues. There are rookie cards for each team each year. Just collecting rookie cards is fun. Another excellent idea is to collect all of the players' cards of a new team. Several years from now, your cards will increase in value as these starters are traded to other teams.

Some collectors like to have their cards autographed and some do not. Those that do, don't think having a player sign a card defaces it. Some cards increase in value by having an autograph, and it's fun to meet the players as you get their autograph.

The first cards were printed in 1887 and came in packs of cigarettes with names like "Old Judge," "Gypsy Queen," and "Dogs Head." Soon candy makers began putting them in their packages to sell more candy. Then bubble gum manufacturers included them with packs of gum, and more people began collecting them. Now the cards are sold separately and are no longer free with your gum. The player's picture is on the front of the card, and all of his baseball statistics are on the back, including all of the teams with which he has played.

You can buy, sell, or trade baseball cards in stores, flea markets, auctions, garage sales, and card shows. Sometimes famous players are at stores and card shows to autograph their cards. They usually charge for their signature, but sometimes they will sign free cards and other baseball equipment at the ballpark or other events. Cards are sold individually, in packs of six to 20, or in sets of 132 to 900. A player's card sells for more in his hometown. This is called "above book" price. There are books in stores and libraries that tell you how much each card is worth in general. You can find the books in the library or in card stores. A lot of other stores have baseball cards. You'll see them on convenience store and department store shelves, even at the check-out stand in food markets.

You can usually find a card club to join in your neighborhood or at school. If you don't have one, start your own. You could invite all your friends for a "card party" and organize a swap meet, or you could organize one with your teacher to be held during break time or after school.

GO ON

READING PRACTICE TEST
Part 2: Comprehension (cont.)

8. **The main idea of this selection is —**

   (F) baseball cards have become larger in size than they were many years ago.

   (G) collecting baseball cards is a great hobby.

   (H) it's better to sell cards than to buy them.

   (J) autographed baseball cards are not worth very much.

9. **Which of these statements is true?**

   (A) Almost all superstars charge for signing their cards.

   (B) The first baseball cards were printed in 1877.

   (C) Baseball cards usually come in a package with bubble gum.

   (D) All baseball cards increase in value with age.

10. **Which of these conclusions can you draw from reading the passage?**

    (F) It would be great to own a Honus Wagner baseball card!

    (G) Everyone loves collecting baseball cards.

    (H) The older the card, the greater the value.

    (J) Rookie cards seldom have much value.

11. **Baseball cards of today can be found in all of the following except—**

    (A) convenience stores.

    (B) sports card stores.

    (C) food stores.

    (D) appliance stores.

12. **The first baseball cards were distributed in —**

    (F) packs of bubble gum.

    (G) packs of cigarettes.

    (H) packs of loose candy pieces.

    (J) packages of potato chips.

13. **The term "above book" refers to —**

    (A) secret prices for baseball cards.

    (B) cards selling for more than their estimated value.

    (C) prices that are determined by Las Vegas.

    (D) entire books of baseball cards.

14. **On the backside of each baseball card is usually —**

    (F) nothing.

    (G) the current major league standings.

    (H) the player's statistics at the time it was printed.

    (J) a schedule of this year's games where the player can be seen.

STOP

LANGUAGE: MECHANICS

● **Lesson 1: Punctuation**

Directions: Mark the space for the punctuation mark that is needed in the sentence.
Mark the space for "none" if no more punctuation marks are needed.

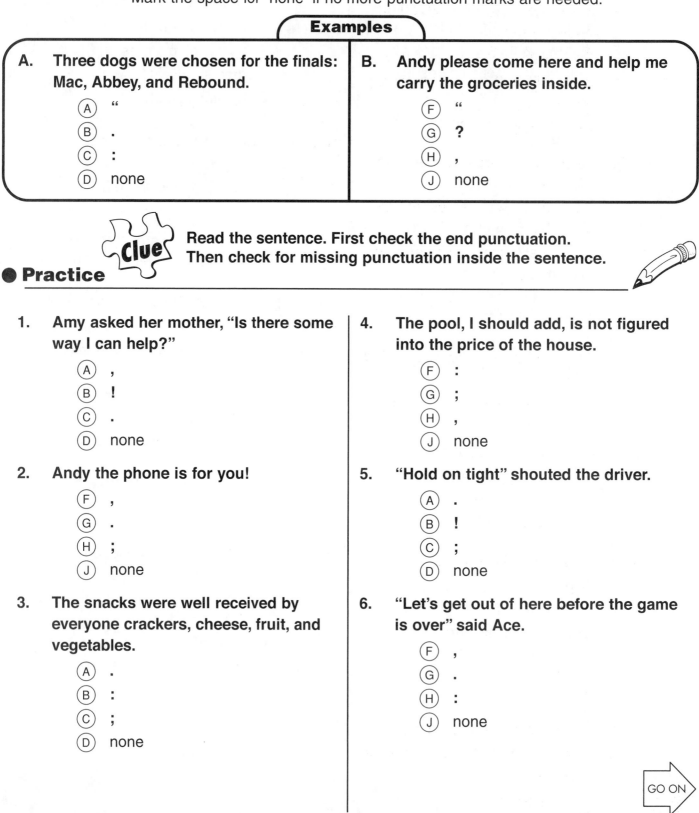

Examples

A. Three dogs were chosen for the finals:
Mac, Abbey, and Rebound.

(A) "
(B) .
(C) :
(D) none

B. Andy please come here and help me
carry the groceries inside.

(F) "
(G) ?
(H) ,
(J) none

Clue Read the sentence. First check the end punctuation.
Then check for missing punctuation inside the sentence.

● **Practice**

1. Amy asked her mother, "Is there some
way I can help?"

(A) ,
(B) !
(C) .
(D) none

2. Andy the phone is for you!

(F) ,
(G) .
(H) ;
(J) none

3. The snacks were well received by
everyone crackers, cheese, fruit, and
vegetables.

(A) .
(B) :
(C) ;
(D) none

4. The pool, I should add, is not figured
into the price of the house.

(F) :
(G) ;
(H) ,
(J) none

5. "Hold on tight" shouted the driver.

(A) .
(B) !
(C) ;
(D) none

6. "Let's get out of here before the game
is over" said Ace.

(F) ,
(G) .
(H) :
(J) none

GO ON

LANGUAGE: MECHANICS

● Lesson 1: Punctuation (cont.)

For numbers 7–13, read each answer. Fill in the space for the choice that has a punctuation error. If there is no mistake, fill in the fourth answer space.

7.
- (A) People should be more careful
- (B) when driving their cars in a parking
- (C) garage to avoid hitting others.
- (D) (no mistakes)

8.
- (F) Cacti, palo verde and mesquite were all
- (G) thriving in the desert despite the lack of rain
- (H) and water from any other source.
- (J) (no mistakes)

9.
- (A) While the school year is not yet over
- (B) many of the students are already planning
- (C) fun things to do for the summer.
- (D) (no mistakes)

10.
- (F) CDO High School
- (G) 122 Calle Concordia
- (H) Tucson, AZ 85737
- (J) (no mistakes)

11.
- (A) Please send me a copy of your most
- (B) recent catalog of summer programs that
- (C) are available for the coming summer
- (D) (no mistakes)

12.
- (F) I look forward to your visit as
- (G) I have lots of fun things planned for
- (H) us to do.
- (J) (no mistakes)

13.
- (A) Wittier College
- (B) Benson Pak, IA 60610
- (C) Dear Dr Adams:
- (D) (no mistakes)

For numbers 14–17, read each sentence. Choose the word or words that fit best in the blank and show the correct punctuation.

14. **After you finish this _____ I will ask you to go on to the next one.**
- (F) assignment Kim
- (G) assignment, Kim:
- (H) assignment, Kim,
- (J) assignment, Kim

15. **The _____ face was covered with make-up and sweat.**
- (A) actors
- (B) actor's
- (C) actors'
- (D) actors's

16. **_____ wondered Jacob as the party continued on.**
- (F) "Why did they leave early?"
- (G) "Why did they leave early,"
- (H) "Why did they leave early."
- (J) "Why did they leave early"

17. **If you do not bring both your _____ you will not be allowed to participate in the ceremony.**
- (A) cap and gown:
- (B) cap and gown,
- (C) cap and gown;
- (D) cap and gown

STOP

Name _____   Date_____

LANGUAGE: MECHANICS

● **Lesson 2: Capitalization and Punctuation**

Directions: In Example A, mark the space for the answer that shows incorrect punctuation and capitalization. In Example B, mark the space that will correct the underlined words. If the underlined part is correct, mark "Correct as it is."

Examples

A.
- (A) We need to, help each other
- (B) Don't be afraid to stay after dark.
- (C) This shouldn't be too heavy a burden.
- (D) We can't paint the table until it's dry.

B. If people <u>care enough, we can win.</u>
- (F) care enough. We
- (G) care enough we,
- (H) care enough; we
- (J) correct as it is

Clue If you are not sure which answer is correct, take your best guess. Eliminate answer choices you know are wrong.

● **Practice**

For numbers 1–2, mark the space of the choice that is correct as written. For numbers 3–6, mark the choice that corresponds to the correction of the underlined words.

1.
- (A) Stuart said in disbelief, "he is juggling eight flaming swords."
- (B) "I wonder," puzzled Rose, "Why he doesn't fall from the high wire."
- (C) Mark said, "They must have trained for years to be so good."
- (D) "Watching the trapeze artists, said Rachel, makes me nervous."

2.
- (F) The meeting; will be on Tuesday.
- (G) Gina is president. Until the next election.
- (H) Everyone, at the meeting, is a member.
- (J) If you are late, we'll start without you.

3. We <u>arent</u> ready to leave.
- (A) arent'
- (B) are'nt
- (C) aren't
- (D) correct as it is

4. <u>Rabbits, cats, and squirrels</u> have four legs.
- (F) Rabbits. Cats, and squirrels
- (G) Rabbits, cats and humans
- (H) Rabbits, cats and, squirrels
- (J) correct as it is

5. <u>Hurry</u>
- (A) Hurry!
- (B) Hurry.
- (C) Hurry;
- (D) correct as it is

6. The <u>balls and tees</u> were in the golf bag.
- (F) balls, and tees
- (G) balls and, tees
- (H) balls, and, tees
- (J) correct as it is

GO ON

1-57768-978-X *Spectrum Test Practice 8*

LANGUAGE: MECHANICS
● Lesson 2: Capitalization and Punctuation (cont.)

For numbers 7–14, read the paragraph and the underlined parts. Choose the answer that shows the best capitalization and punctuation for each part.

Director of Subscription Services

Hikers & Campers
(7) p.o. box 2326
(8) Chicago, Illinois, 60613

Dear Director:
I have not received the last two issues of Hikers & Campers magazine. I request that you extend my **(9)** current subscription, for two months to make up for the two issues I missed. I would appreciate your help in solving this problem.
(10)   sincerely:
        Tomas Fisher

7. Ⓐ P.O. Box, 2326
    Ⓑ P.O. box 2326
    Ⓒ P.O. Box 2326
    Ⓓ correct as it is

8. Ⓕ Chicago, Illinois 60613
    Ⓖ Chicago Illinois 60613
    Ⓗ Chicago Illinois, 60613
    Ⓙ correct as it is

9. Ⓐ current, subscription
    Ⓑ current, subscription,
    Ⓒ current subscription
    Ⓓ correct as it is

10. Ⓕ Sincerely,
    Ⓖ sincerely;
    Ⓗ Sincerely
    Ⓙ correct as it is

Read the passage below and correct numbers 11–15 by making the choice that will correctly punctuate the underlined words.

One of the newest ways of keeping a house warm is radiant **(11)** heating coils of plastic tubing are built into the floor or slab of the house. When it becomes necessary to heat the **(12)** house hot water is forced through the tubing. The floor becomes warm, and because heat rises, so does the air in the rest of **(13)** the house. It is an efficient heating **(14)** system. That is becoming more and more popular.

11. Ⓐ heating, coils
    Ⓑ heating. Coils
    Ⓒ heating: Coils
    Ⓓ correct as it is

12. Ⓕ house, hot
    Ⓖ house. Hot
    Ⓗ House. Hot
    Ⓙ correct as it is

13. Ⓐ the house, it
    Ⓑ the House, it
    Ⓒ the house; it
    Ⓓ correct as it is

14. Ⓕ system, that
    Ⓖ system; that
    Ⓗ system that
    Ⓙ correct as it is

GO ON

LANGUAGE: MECHANICS

● Lesson 2: Capitalization and Punctuation (cont.)

Read each sentence. Decide which word that is not capitalized should be capitalized. Fill in the circle that corresponds to the incorrect part of the sentence. If there are no errors, mark "correct as is."

15. In april, the mayor will run again for office.

(A) In april

(B) the mayor

(C) will run again for office.

(D) correct as is

16. my sister and I went to the movie.

(F) my sister

(G) and I

(H) went to the movie.

(J) correct as is

17. Have you seen any movies by steven Spielberg?

(A) Have you

(B) seen any movies

(C) by steven Spielberg?

(D) correct as is

18. The atlantic Ocean is the second largest ocean in the world.

(F) The atlantic

(G) Ocean is the second largest

(H) in the world.

(J) correct as it

19. the street was recently resurfaced with asphalt.

(A) the

(B) street was recently resurfaced

(C) with asphalt.

(D) correct as it

20. In venice, the streets are canals.

(F) In venice,

(G) the streets

(H) are canals.

(J) correct as is

21. Benjamin franklin once said, "a penny saved is a penny earned."

(A) Benjamin franklin once said, "a

(B) penny saved

(C) is a penny earned."

(D) correct as is

22. Black beauty is a story about a horse.

(F) Black beauty

(G) is a story

(H) about a horse.

(J) correct as is

23. Many homes in the desert have swimming pools.

(A) Many homes

(B) in the desert

(C) have swimming pools.

(D) correct as is

24. Those who attended the elks dance seemed to enjoy themselves very much.

(F) Those who attended the elks

(G) dance

(H) seemed to enjoy themselves very much.

(J) correct as is

STOP

LANGUAGE: MECHANICS
SAMPLE TEST

● **Directions:** Fill in the answer choice for the punctuation that is needed in the sentence. If no punctuation is needed, fill in the answer choice for "none."

Example

A.   "We must try harder" yelled the coach at his young team during the halftime intermission.

   Ⓐ ,
   Ⓑ .
   Ⓒ !
   Ⓓ none

---

1.   **Some Canadians speak both English and French.**

   Ⓐ ,
   Ⓑ .
   Ⓒ !
   Ⓓ none

2.   **Wendy can you help me to move this picture?**

   Ⓕ ,
   Ⓖ .
   Ⓗ ?
   Ⓙ none

3.   **In school she played studied and sometimes went out on dates.**

   Ⓐ ,
   Ⓑ .
   Ⓒ ?
   Ⓓ none

4.   **Jonathan, will you please try to be home in time for dinner**

   Ⓕ ,
   Ⓖ .
   Ⓗ ?
   Ⓙ none

For numbers 5–7 read each answer. Fill in the space of the sentence with correct punctuation.

5.   Ⓐ The alarm clock rang at 7:15 A.M.
     Ⓑ I stayed in bed, until 7:30 A.M.
     Ⓒ At 8:15 A.M. I caught the school bus?
     Ⓓ The alarm rang, again at 7:15 P.M.

6.   Ⓕ Corn is grown in Indiana, Iowa, and Illinois.
     Ⓖ Potatoes are products of Idaho Maine, and Long Island.
     Ⓗ Oranges are a major crop in California Florida and Texas.
     Ⓙ Wheat is a major crop in Kansas, over Nebraska

7.   Ⓐ Tenth St
     Ⓑ Maple Ave
     Ⓒ Ash Dr.
     Ⓓ Eagle Peak Dr

GO ON

LANGUAGE: MECHANICS
SAMPLE TEST (cont.)

For numbers 8 and 9 choose the word or words that best fit the blank and show the correct punctuation.

8. Matt, _____ received a perfect score on his math test.

   F not Mike,
   G not Mike
   H not Mike:
   J not, Mike

9. Please turn on the air conditioner _____ it's 85 degrees in here!

   A because,
   B because:
   C because
   D because;

For numbers 10–13, read each group of sentences. Find the one that is written correctly and shows the correct capitalization and punctuation.

10. F Let's move away from here before we get wet,
    G The new sofa is now in the garage?
    H Do you realize that the front door is open?
    J The hammer and Nails aren't where you said they should be.

11. A Disneyland, is visited by many tourists from other Countries.
    B If you visit venice italy, be sure to ride on a gondola.
    C If you go to the County fair, be sure you take plenty of money.
    D What time of day do you think we should go to the polls?

12. F I was late for class, but everyone else was on time.
    G Randy and Angie, arrived yesterday.
    H The suitcases are packed, and are in the trunk of the car.
    J Summer can be fun but, only if you plan it right.

13. A Courtney reminded Garrett, "That he promised to help."
    B We should buy some fruit trees, and plant them in the backyard" suggested Lillian.
    C "The city council has given us permission, added Robert
    D "Did you remember to bring your rocket?" asked Tim.

For numbers 14–15, read the passage. Find the answer choice that shows the correct capitalization and punctuation for the underlined part.

   "Are you sure this is the right **(14)** pattern?" asked Carolyn. She looked at the tiles the **(15)** carpenter's had already completed and then at the sample.

14. F pattern," asked
    G pattern, "Asked
    H pattern asked"
    J correct as it is

15. A carpenters had
    B carpenters' had
    C carpenters, had
    D correct as it is

STOP

Name _____   Date _____

LANGUAGE: EXPRESSION

● **Lesson 3: Usage**

Directions: Read each sentence. Find the word or phrase that best completes the sentence.

Examples

A. Everyone _____ to be first in line for the movie.

  (A) wanting
  (B) will wants
  (C) want
  (D) wants

B. As we had hoped, the magic trick worked _____.

  (F) perfect
  (G) perfectly
  (H) more perfect
  (J) most perfectly

Clue If you are not sure which answer is correct, take your best guess. Say each answer choice to yourself or try each answer in the blank and say the completed sentence to yourself.

● **Practice**

For numbers 1–3, choose the word or phrase that best completes the sentence.

1. **This is the garden _____ Angie planted last spring.**

  (A) who
  (B) that
  (C) them
  (D) where

2. **Everything you need is on the table, so please make _____ sandwiches.**

  (F) you
  (G) herself
  (H) yourself
  (J) theirselves

3. **Open a window so we can get some _____ air in this room.**

  (A) fresh
  (B) freshly
  (C) freshest
  (D) most fresh

For numbers 4–6, choose the answer that is a correctly written sentence.

4. (F) Stop by the store and pick up milk and bread.

  (G) The street covered with leaves from the trees.

  (H) Hold the paper, please I'll staple it together.

  (J) The radio and television from Warner's.

5. (A) This is the earlier bus has arrived.

  (B) The most best basketball player in the school is Heidi McLain.

  (C) Very fewest of us had gone water skiing before.

  (D) A bright light flashed in the sky.

6. (F) When us went home, we found a big surprise.

  (G) Let's give them some of the corn from our garden.

  (H) His was not sure when it happened.

  (J) I couldn't believe it was actually happening to I.

GO ON

LANGUAGE: EXPRESSION

● Lesson 3: Usage (cont.)

For numbers 7–12, read each answer choice. Fill in the space for the part of the sentence that has a usage error. If there is no mistake, fill in the fourth answer space.

7.
- Ⓐ The end result of the meeting
- Ⓑ was that no decisions were
- Ⓒ made whatsoever!
- Ⓓ no mistakes

8.
- Ⓕ If I followed you around all day
- Ⓖ long, I'm sure I would be wore
- Ⓗ out by the end of the day.
- Ⓙ no mistakes

9.
- Ⓐ Tommy and me always pick the
- Ⓑ hottest time of day to do
- Ⓒ our chores because we love the heat.
- Ⓓ no mistakes

10.
- Ⓕ The grades I got in school were
- Ⓖ certainly okay with me, but my
- Ⓗ parents said they was unacceptable.
- Ⓙ no mistakes

11.
- Ⓐ The fishes you saw in the river
- Ⓑ were catfish, which are great to eat
- Ⓒ but have lots of little bones.
- Ⓓ no mistakes

12.
- Ⓕ Nixon hit his drive very straight,
- Ⓖ but it went too far and carried through
- Ⓗ the fairway and into the rough.
- Ⓙ no mistakes

For numbers 13 and 14, choose the best way to write the underlined part of each sentence. If the underlined part is correct, fill in the fourth answer space.

13. Traffic on the freeway <u>was heavy</u> because the gem show was in town.
- Ⓐ will be heavy
- Ⓑ can be heavy
- Ⓒ is heavy
- Ⓓ no change

14. <u>Whether</u> it is spring, the trees are not yet budding because it's so cold!
- Ⓕ Although
- Ⓖ Because
- Ⓗ Despite
- Ⓙ no change

For numbers 15 and 16, choose the answer that is a correctly written sentence.

15.
- Ⓐ We gave our dog a bath, but we don't get him very clean.
- Ⓑ The principal give trophies to both of the co-captains.
- Ⓒ The sun shine brightly on the waves.
- Ⓓ Cindy tried knocking at the door one more time.

16.
- Ⓕ Pam receive a digital watch for graduation.
- Ⓖ She send us a dozen oranges from Florida as a gift.
- Ⓗ The unhappy crowd showed its distaste for the concert.
- Ⓙ Our class schedules was printed out on the school computer.

GO ON

● **Lesson 3: Usage (cont.)**

For numbers 17–20, read the following passage, then choose the best answer for each of the questions that follow.

Perks is a term for rewards. They are what some companies give to their employees for doing a good job. **(17)** An <u>example</u> of perks may involve giving an employee who has done a good job actual products. Or the **(18)** <u>employer</u> may be allowed to leave work early or be given an entire day away from work with pay. The perk may give the employee access to the best parking spot for a month or a financial bonus. Perks, or rewards, for a job well done help make people try harder to succeed.

As you continue to work hard and earn the good grades that will **(19)** <u>naturally</u> follow hard work, you will want to consider how you may choose to reward yourself for such good study skills and commitment.

Not all rewards need to be **(20)** <u>more extravagant</u> or cost money. Rewards can involve simple ideas like a break from doing household chores, being granted an extra hour of television time, being allowed extra time to be with your friends, or even having more telephone or video game privileges.

17. **In sentence 2, *example* is best written—**
    - Ⓐ Examples
    - Ⓑ Exampler
    - Ⓒ Examplest
    - Ⓓ As it is

18. **In sentence 3, *employer* is best written—**
    - Ⓕ More the employers
    - Ⓖ employee
    - Ⓗ of the employ
    - Ⓙ As it is

19. **In sentence 6, *naturally* is best written—**
    - Ⓐ more natural
    - Ⓑ most natural
    - Ⓒ most naturally
    - Ⓓ As it is

20. **In sentence 7, *more extravagant* is best written—**
    - Ⓕ extravagantler
    - Ⓖ more extravaganter
    - Ⓗ extravagant
    - Ⓙ As it is

LANGUAGE: EXPRESSION

● Lesson 4: Sentences

Directions: Read the directions for each section. Fill in the circle for the answer you think is correct.

Examples

Choose the simple subject of the sentence.

A. The **(A)** hurricane left **(B)** people **(C)** without **(D)** homes.

- Ⓐ hurricane
- Ⓑ people
- Ⓒ without
- Ⓓ homes

Choose the simple predicate (verb) of the sentence.

B. The barge **(F)** traveled **(G)** down the **(H)** river at a very slow **(J)** speed.

- Ⓕ traveled
- Ⓖ down
- Ⓗ river
- Ⓙ speed

Clue Stay with your first answer choice. You should change an answer only if you are sure the one you chose is wrong.

● Practice

For numbers 1–3, find the simple subject and fill in the circle that corresponds to that choice.

1. The **(A)** detective held the **(B)** suspect in **(C)** custody because of the **(D)** evidence he had found.

- Ⓐ detective
- Ⓑ suspect
- Ⓒ custody
- Ⓓ evidence

2. The **(F)** finalists in the chess **(G)** tournament were from **(H)** Arizona and **(J)** California.

- Ⓕ finalists
- Ⓖ tournament
- Ⓗ Arizona
- Ⓙ California

3. After **(A)** breakfast, **(B)** I usually like to take a **(C)** walk on the **(D)** beach.

- Ⓐ breakfast
- Ⓑ I
- Ⓒ walk
- Ⓓ beach

For numbers 4–6, find the underlined part that is the simple predicate (verb) of the sentence.

4. A **(F)** huge **(G)** stain **(H)** ruined the **(J)** beauty of the dress.

- Ⓕ huge
- Ⓖ stain
- Ⓗ ruined
- Ⓙ beauty

5. **(A)** Visitors to the **(B)** cave **(C)** remove **(D)** all gum before entering.

- Ⓐ Visitors
- Ⓑ cave
- Ⓒ remove
- Ⓓ gum

6. **(F)** War Emblem **(G)** became **(H)** the proud **(J)** winner of the Derby.

- Ⓕ War Emblem
- Ⓖ became
- Ⓗ proud
- Ⓙ winner

GO ON

LANGUAGE EXPRESSION

● Lesson 4: Sentences (cont.)

For numbers 7–9, choose the answer that best combines the sentences.

7. **Cable subscribers do get a discount on a digital installation. They must respond by May 15 to get the discount.**

    Ⓐ If you order the discount, you may become a cable subscriber by May 15.

    Ⓑ There is a discount to cable subscribers, but only if they buy a digital installation.

    Ⓒ Cable subscribers can get a discount on a digital installation if they respond by May 15.

    Ⓓ Responding by May 15 will get you a free digital installation.

8. **We visited a TV studio set last week. We watched them record a talk show.**

    Ⓕ We visited a TV studio set last week because we watched a talk show.

    Ⓖ If we watch a live talk show, we can visit the studio last week.

    Ⓗ We visited a TV studio last week and watched them record a talk show.

    Ⓙ While we were watching a talk show, we then went to a TV studio.

9. **I hooked my drive far to the left. It bounced off the fence between the golf course and the homeowners' property. It bounced off his patio and landed in his swimming pool.**

    Ⓐ Because I hooked my drive, it bounced off the golf course, and landed by a fence.

    Ⓑ Because my golf ball went into a swimming pool, it bounced off a fence between the golf course and a property, then hooked.

    Ⓒ Because I hooked my drive far to the left, it bounced off a fence between the course and private property, and landed in the owner's swimming pool.

    Ⓓ Because the ball bounced off the fence, it then hooked and went into the pool.

For numbers 10 and 11, choose the best way of expressing the idea.

10. Ⓕ Having just finished work on the cabin, the contractor stepped back filled with pride, and admired it.

    Ⓖ Filled with pride, the contractor stepped back and admired the cab he had just built.

    Ⓗ The contractor was filled with pride, stepping back to admire the cabin he had just built.

    Ⓙ The cabin he had just built filled the contractor with pride, so he stepped back and admired it.

11. Ⓐ Ryan wasn't certain what time the game started, so he called the ticket office.

    Ⓑ Calling the ticket office, Ryan wasn't certain what time the game started.

    Ⓒ Because he called the ticket office, Ryan wasn't sure what time the game started.

    Ⓓ Although he wasn't sure what time the game started, Ryan called the ticket office.

GO ON

LANGUAGE EXPRESSION

● Lesson 4: Sentences (cont.)

Read the following passage and then choose the best answer for each question that follows.

(1) A hurricane is a form of a cyclone, a tornado is another. (2) A cyclone is a region that is surrounded by a rotating wind system. (3) But the characteristics of each differ greatly. (4) A hurricane is like a huge machine. (5) It keeps the planet's temperature in balance by moving hot air from the tropics into the middle latitudes. (6) Meteorologists study tropical storms and general weather patterns. (7) They develop an understanding of hurricanes. (8) They predict their formation, duration, and path. (9) A tornado is like a concentrated hurricane that forms over land. (10) Reach speeds twice that of a hurricane's

12. Which of these sentences is a run-on sentence?

- (F) 1
- (G) 4
- (H) 7
- (J) 8

13. How can sentences 4 and 5 best be combined without changing their meaning?

- (A) A hurricane is like a huge machine that keeps the planet's temperature in balance by moving hot air from the tropics into the middle latitudes.
- (B) If a hurricane is a huge machine, it can keep the hot air moving out of the tropics.
- (C) The planet's temperature is

balanced because by moving hot air, the hurricane is a machine.

- (D) A huge machine called a hurricane moves hot air into the tropics from the middle latitudes, making it balanced.

14. How can sentences 6 and 7 be made better?

- (F) Meteorologists study hurricanes and they understand hurricane weather systems.
- (G) By studying tropical storms and general weather patterns, meteorologists have developed an understanding of hurricanes.
- (H) Because meteorologists study hurricanes, weather patterns develop their understanding of how they happen.
- (J) Meteorologists study hurricane weather systems and should understand their development.

15. Which of these is not a sentence?

- (A) 2
- (B) 4
- (C) 6
- (D) 10

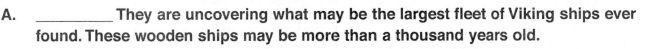

LANGUAGE: EXPRESSION

● Lesson 5: Paragraphs

Directions: Find the best topic sentence for the example below.

Example

A. _____ They are uncovering what may be the largest fleet of Viking ships ever found. These wooden ships may be more than a thousand years old.

- (A) Viking pirates were most active during the Middle Ages.
- (B) Scientists are digging up history off the coast of Denmark.
- (C) The Vikings were pirates who lived in Norway, Sweden, and Denmark.
- (D) The ships are being brought up piece by piece from the bottom of the sea.

 **Clue** Remember, a paragraph should focus on one idea. The correct answer is the one that fits best with the rest of the paragraph.

● Practice

Read the paragraph below. Then find the best topic sentence for that paragraph from the choices following the paragraph.

1. _____ Abraham Lincoln learned to live with the many nicknames he was given. Those nicknames included Honest Abe and the Rail Splitter. Most of them he accepted in good humor, but he did not like the name Ape, which referred to his gangly appearance.

- (A) The nicknames of famous Presidents were given by their close friends.
- (B) Abraham Lincoln was arguably the best President ever.
- (C) Nicknames are signs of a President's popularity.
- (D) Like it or not, many of our Presidents were not always addressed by their given name.

Find the answer choice that best develops the topic sentence below.

2. _____ People who live in the desert often find great relief and joy from a summer thunderstorm.

- (F) The rain in the desert is needed all year long, but especially during the summer months.
- (G) Many people like watching the power of Mother Nature found in a thunderstorm and often just sit back and enjoy.
- (H) While the rain is pelting down on the desert floor, many people begin worrying about the possibility of flash floods.
- (J) The desert is a place of peace and serenity, especially during a thunderstorm.

 GO ON

LANGUAGE: EXPRESSION

● **Lesson 5: Paragraphs (cont.)**

For numbers 3 and 4, read the paragraph. Find the sentence that does not belong in the paragraph.

3.   **(1)** In the early 1790s, Catherine Littlefield Greene had a brainstorm. **(2)** She found that cotton seeds could be removed mechanically by catching the cotton fibers and letting the seeds fall through. **(3)** Because she was a high society lady, she was not supposed to associate herself with such dirty machines. **(4)** Her life was much more comfortable before she married.

    (A) sentence 1
    (B) sentence 2
    (C) sentence 3
    (D) sentence 4

4.   **(1)** Mary Livermore was the wife of a Chicago minister. **(2)** Mary Livermore's work involved establishing over three thousand chapters of the United States Sanitary Commission. **(3)** The organization's success included providing Union soldiers with a continual supply of fresh vegetables. **(4)** The vegetables were said to have saved the troops of General Grant from a scurvy epidemic.

    (F) sentence 1
    (G) sentence 2
    (H) sentence 3
    (J) sentence 4

For numbers 5 and 6, read the paragraph. Find the sentence that best fits the blank in the paragraph.

5.   The artifacts of the ancient Mayan civilizations were first uncovered in 1839 by John Lloyd Stephens. _____. Scientists and historians flocked to the jungles of southern Mexico and surrounding areas. They were trying to determine who the Mayans were, when their culture thrived, and why it eventually collapsed.

    (A) Most Mayans came originally from South America.
    (B) Word of his discovery spread like wildfire.
    (C) The Mayan culture was very sophisticated for its day.
    (D) Many Mayan mysteries remain unsolved today.

6.   Ancient sculptors made many bronze pieces to decorate their temples. The sculptor always began the art by carving a figure out of wax and dipping it into a mixture of clay and water. _____. The sculptor then poured liquid bronze into the mold to complete the final piece.

    (F) Wax cut from the figure could be melted and used again.
    (G) Many of the statues were larger than actual life-size.
    (H) The figure was baked to melt the wax and leave a hollow clay mold.
    (J) Bronze had to be heated to a very hot temperature to melt it down.

GO ON

LANGUAGE: EXPRESSION

● Lesson 5: Paragraphs (cont.)

For numbers 7–9, use the paragraph below to answer the questions.

(1) One of the most fascinating figures on ancient artifacts is that of Kokopelli. (2) Kokopelli is compelling, not only because he is cute and vibrant, but because he is everywhere. (3) Several Native American tribes, including the Hopi, Zuni, Winnebago, and Anasazi, tell stories and depict images of the flute playing, hunch-backed little man. (4) Each tribe's idea of just who Kokopelli was is a little different. (5) Kokopelli T-shirts are very popular in the Southwest.

7. **Choose the best opening sentence to add to this paragraph.**

(A) Native Americans loved Kokopelli because he played a flute.

(B) Native Americans chronicled their lives and their myths through the ancient inscriptions and pictographs found on the artifacts of their culture.

(C) Images of Kokopelli are found on jewelry, key chains, and T-shirts all over the Southwest.

(D) Southwestern Native Americans worshipped characters like Kokopelli because they loved his music.

8. **Which sentence should be left out of this paragraph?**

(F) sentence 1

(G) sentence 2

(H) sentence 4

(J) sentence 5

9. **Where is the best place for sentence 4?**

(A) Where it is now

(B) Between sentences 1 and 2

(C) Between sentences 2 and 3

(D) Before sentence 1

10. **Which of the following would be most appropriate to include in the beginning of a report on the Declaration of Independence?**

(F) The various parts of the Declaration of Independence fall in a most logical order once you know what the document was all about. It was the combination of a lot of ideas that were generated by some pretty smart guys.

(G) The original document was written by Thomas Jefferson, but he used the ideas of several of his friends and also the ideas of those who were attending the convention. His ideas are timeless because he worked very late at night to meet the deadline getting the document written.

(H) The Declaration of Independence is regarded by historians as one of the most beautifully written documents of all time. It became the symbol of freedom for the colonists in their war against England.

(J) If the Declaration of Independence had been shorter in length, most probably it would have been read by more people.

GO ON

Name _____   Date_____

● Lesson 5: Paragraphs (cont.)

Read the following passage. Then answer questions 11–14 by choosing the best answer to each question.

(1) Elements of science fiction can be found in stories dating as far back as ancient Babylonia. (2) The Babylonians were not very skilled in athletics. (3) Some early Greek and Roman literature related tales of curious voyages and encounters with strange beings.

(4) The Industrial Revolution gave birth to modern science-fiction themes and styles. (5) Intrigued with the remarkable changes going on around them, novelists began to write about science in earnest. (6) The first specialist in the genre was Jules Verne.

(7) Verne wrote such well-researched and fascinating tales that they became the prototype for science-fiction stories to follow. (8) Many scientists from the past and present have credited his words for motivating them to become involved in their profession.

11. Which sentence should be placed before sentence 1?

- (A) Science-fiction themes are purely for entertainment, and never have any bearing on actual events.
- (B) Science-fiction themes include space and time travel, alien invasions, and crises created by technology gone awry.
- (C) Jules Verne's childhood inspired him to become a writer that few people know about.
- (D) Technological advances have made science fiction almost non-existent today.

12. Which sentence does not belong in the passage?

- (F) sentence 2
- (G) sentence 3
- (H) sentence 5
- (J) sentence 7

13. What supporting information could be added before sentence 6?

- (A) Technology was far down the road, so much of the early techniques lacked any kind of drama.
- (B) Edgar Allen Poe, Mark Twain, and Nathaniel Hawthorne all dabbled in science-fiction writing.
- (C) Had Jules Verne not entered into science-fiction writing, he probably wouldn't have become very famous.
- (D) Research and science fiction have a lot in common as we know today.

14. Which sentence tells us the big reason for the success of Jules Verne?

- (F) sentence 1
- (G) sentence 4
- (H) sentence 6
- (J) sentence 7

STOP

LANGUAGE: EXPRESSION
SAMPLE TEST

● **Directions:** Choose the best answer for each of the following by filling in the circle that corresponds to that answer.

Example

Find the simple subject in the following sentence.

A.   The **(A)** anxious **(B)** wives **(C)** awaited the safe return of the **(D)** astronauts.

- Ⓐ anxious
- Ⓑ wives
- Ⓒ awaited
- Ⓓ astronauts

For number 1, choose the word or phrase that best completes the sentence.

1.   _____ will be home late for dinner tonight because we must go to the library to work on our presentation.

- Ⓐ I and Chris
- Ⓑ Chris and me
- Ⓒ Chris and I
- Ⓓ Me and Chris

For number 2, choose the answer that is a complete and correctly written sentence.

2.   Ⓕ The water makes the grass grow but then we had to mow.
     Ⓖ Our new mower runs much better than the old one.
     Ⓗ I cannot mow the lawn unless someone went to get me some more gas.
     Ⓙ The electric starter makes is more easier to get the mower started.

For numbers 3–5, read each answer choice. Fill in the space for the choice that has a usage error. If there is no mistake, fill in the fourth answer space.

3.   Ⓐ We had to place film on the windows
     Ⓑ twice because the first time
     Ⓒ we didn't apply it correctly.
     Ⓓ no mistakes

4.   Ⓕ Taxes in our city are very high
     Ⓖ because the city council is trying
     Ⓗ to improve our system of roads.
     Ⓙ no mistakes

5.   Ⓐ I wanted to claim the puppy with
     Ⓑ the fluffy head, but someone went and
     Ⓒ claimed her before I arrived.
     Ⓓ no mistakes

For number 6, find the underlined part that is the simple subject of the sentence.

6.   This **(F)** time **(G)** I plan to **(H)** throw the ball over the **(J)** fence.

- Ⓕ time
- Ⓖ I
- Ⓗ throw
- Ⓙ fence

GO ON ⇨

For number 7, find the underlined word that is the simple predicate (verb) of the sentence.

7. **(A)** Jamie and her roommate **(B)** jumped into the **(C)** hotel swimming pool at the same **(D)** time.

  - (A) Jamie
  - (B) jumped
  - (C) hotel
  - (D) time

For numbers 8–10, choose the answer that best combines the underlined sentences.

8. **The student brought the apples to school. The student gave an apple to each classmate.**

  - (F) The student gave apples to his classmates.
  - (G) The student brought the apples to school and gave one to each classmate.
  - (H) The student brought the apples to school and gave an apple to each classmate.
  - (J) The student brought the apples to school because his classmates wanted them.

9. **The Sahara Desert has nearly 100 large oases. An oasis is a place with water.**

  - (A) The Sahara Desert has nearly 100 oases, with water.
  - (B) The Sahara Desert has nearly 100 large oases—places with water.
  - (C) There are nearly 100 large oases of water in the Sahara Desert.
  - (D) The Sahara Desert has nearly 100 large places with water, oases.

10. **My mom was sick today. We did not go shopping.**

  - (F) Today my mom was sick, and we did not go shopping.
  - (G) My mom was sick today so we did not go shopping.
  - (H) My mom, today was sick because we did not go shopping.
  - (J) My mom was sick, and today we did not go shopping.

For numbers 11 and 12, choose the best way of expressing the idea.

11.
  - (A) The camera you want is not in this store, although they do sell them.
  - (B) The store has cameras that the camera store does not want you to buy.
  - (C) This store, which has camera, although not the kind you want.
  - (D) Although not the kind of camera you really want to buy, the store does have them.

12.
  - (F) The Charters of Freedom are promptly put to bed every night at Washington, D.C.
  - (G) Every night at the National Archives in Washington, D.C., the Charters of Freedom are promptly put to bed.
  - (H) Every night the Charters of Freedom go to bed promptly in Washington, D.C., when they are told to go.
  - (J) Washington, D.C. is the home to both the National Archives and the Charters of Freedom.

LANGUAGE: EXPRESSION
SAMPLE TEST (cont.)

Read the paragraph below. Find the best topic sentence for the paragraph.

13. _____ The index is an alphabetical listing of the main topics treated in a book. Subtopics are listed alphabetically under the main topics. The pages on which information can be found are indicated alongside the topic.

    (A) The index to a daily newspaper fills many books.

    (B) Index cards are handy for taking notes from an encyclopedia.

    (C) A good reader knows how to use an index.

    (D) An index is useful for locating specific information in a book.

Read the sentence below. Find the best supporting sentence.

14. **Muscles connected to your skeleton are called voluntary muscles.**

    (F) Muscles always work in pairs so joints can move in different directions.

    (G) The human skeleton contains over two hundred bones. Sixty-four of these are found in the arms and hands.

    (H) This means they are under your direct control. You can move these muscles almost any way you want to.

    (J) Some muscles are not connected to your skeleton. For example, your heart contains muscles, but you cannot control their movement.

Read the paragraph below. Find the sentence that does not belong in the paragraph.

15. **(1)** The initials FDR are among the most famous in all of American history. **(2)** While millions of Americans loved him, some did not like him at all. **(3)** He was born into a wealthy family. **(4)** Franklin Delano Roosevelt was president of the United States longer than any other man.

    (A) sentence 1

    (B) sentence 2

    (C) sentence 3

    (D) sentence 4

Read the paragraph below. Find the sentence that best fits the blank in the paragraph.

16. **When John Parke Custis, Martha Washington's son by her first marriage, died, the Washingtons raised his two youngest children. Just before George and Martha married, Washington legally adopted the girl, but he did not adopt her brother. _____ George Washington Parke Custis (the son Washington did not adopt) began building Arlington House on 1100 acres of land owned by his father. Today that land is Arlington National Cemetery.**

    (F) Washington did not adopt the boy because he thought it might affect his claim to the Custis estate.

    (G) Washington wanted a cemetery.

    (H) If Martha had not died when she did, Arlington National Cemetery would probably have not become a reality.

    (J) George Washington Parke Custis married Mary Lee Fitzhugh in Washington, D.C.

GO ON

LANGUAGE: EXPRESSION
SAMPLE TEST (cont.)

Read the following passage then use it to help you choose the correct answers to questions 17–20.

(1) It was on September 19, 1870, at a campfire in Yellowstone, that the idea of a national park was actually born. (2) While seated around the fire, a group of men discussed what should be done to save forever this outstanding country they had been exploring. (3) Some suggested staking out personal claims, but Cornelius Hedges suggested that Yellowstone's unique beauty should belong to all the people as a national park. (4) Other men thought this was a great idea and pledged their support of the measure before Congress. (5) In 1871 an expedition under Dr. Ferdinand Hayden of the U.S. Geological Society visited Yellowstone. (6) He took with him a photographer named William H. Jackson. (7) Members of Congress found his pictures on their desks when they assembled to debate the establishment of Yellowstone as a park. (8) The impact of Jackson's photographs no doubt played a major role in the future of Yellowstone. (9) A great victory for Dr. Hayden.

17. **In sentence 2, <u>save forever</u> is best written—**
    - (A) preserve
    - (B) extend beyond time
    - (C) domesticate
    - (D) As it is

18. **How is sentence 4 best written?**
    - (F) While other men thought this was also a good idea, they pledged their support of the measure before Congress.
    - (G) Congress supported the measure because it was such a good idea of Hedges.
    - (H) Because it was such a great idea, Hedges himself thought it should be brought up before Congress.
    - (J) As it is

19. **Which of these sentences would best follow sentence 6?**
    - (A) Jackson was a former still life photographer, which is why he was commissioned by Dr. Hayden.
    - (B) Most photographers at the time preferred shooting portraits to nature photography.
    - (C) Dr. Hayes' instructions to Jackson were to try to catch some wildlife in action.
    - (D) Jackson's photographs captured the splendor of the country and the drama of the exploration.

20. **Which group of words is not a sentence?**
    - (F) sentence 2
    - (G) sentence 5
    - (H) sentence 6
    - (J) sentence 9

STOP

LANGUAGE: SPELLING

● Lesson 6: Spelling Skills

Directions: Follow the directions for each section. Choose the answer you think is correct.

Examples

Find the word that is spelled correctly and fits best in the blank

A.   What time will be _____ to you?

(A)   acceptible

(B)   acceptable

(C)   accaptable

(D)   acceptabel

B.   Choose the phrase in which the underlined word is not spelled correctly.

(F)   <u>dangerous</u> ride

(G)   small <u>broshure</u>

(H)   important <u>bulletin</u>

(J)   <u>bouquet</u> of flowers

Clue Read the directions carefully. Be sure you know if you are looking for the correctly spelled or incorrectly spelled word.

● Practice

For numbers 1–4, find the word that is spelled correctly and fits best in the blank.

1.   The gas _____ registered empty.

(A)   gage

(B)   geaug

(C)   gauge

(D)   guage

2.   The move was absolutely _____!

(F)   funtastic

(G)   fantactus

(H)   fantasteic

(J)   fantastic

3.   The _____ was heard for miles.

(A)   exploision

(B)   explosen

(C)   explosan

(D)   explosion

4.   She read the poem in an _____ voice.

(F)   expresive

(G)   exprissive

(H)   expressive

(J)   espressive

For numbers 5–7, choose the phrase in which the underlined word is <u>not</u> spelled correctly.

5.   (A)   gasoline <u>monopoly</u>

(B)   <u>multiplication</u> tables

(C)   basic <u>necesity</u>

(D)   art <u>museum</u>

6.   (F)   she wore <u>mocassins</u>

(G)   the <u>murmur</u> of voices

(H)   Greek <u>mythology</u>

(J)   <u>institutions</u> of learning

7.   (A)   <u>investigate</u> the scene

(B)   <u>invasion</u> of the aliens

(C)   a sweet <u>ingredient</u>

(D)   a <u>greade</u> influence

GO ON

LANGUAGE: SPELLING

● Lesson 6: Spelling Skills (cont.)

For numbers 8–10, read each answer. Fill in the space for the choice that has a spelling error. If there is no mistake, fill in the last answer space.

8.
- (F) scissors
- (G) sherrif
- (H) shroud
- (J) (no mistakes)

9.
- (A) steadiest
- (B) scholar
- (C) security
- (D) (no mistakes)

10.
- (F) sargeant
- (G) significant
- (H) specific
- (J) (no mistakes)

For numbers 11–13, read each phrase. One of the underlined words is not spelled correctly for the way it is used in the phrase. Fill in the space for the word that is <u>not</u> spelled correctly.

11.
- (A) breakfast <u>role</u>
- (B) <u>stir</u> the soup
- (C) <u>hand</u> it to Molly
- (D) <u>hop</u> the table

12.
- (F) <u>grove</u> of trees
- (G) <u>angle</u> of ascent
- (H) <u>bread</u> and butter
- (J) <u>cent</u> of victory

13.
- (A) starring <u>role</u>
- (B) <u>scent</u> of flowers
- (C) <u>bred</u> the horses
- (D) <u>vauge</u> response

For numbers 14–17, find the underlined word that is misspelled. If all the words are spelled correctly, mark the space <u>no mistake</u>.

14. Your **(F)** <u>behavior</u> during the **(G)** <u>interim</u> was **(H)** <u>unacceptable</u>. **(J)** no mistake
- (F) behavior
- (G) interim
- (H) unacceptable
- (J) no mistake

15. The **(A)** <u>professional</u> baseball player's **(B)** <u>autograf</u> was **(C)** <u>authentic</u>. **(D)** no mistake
- (A) professional
- (B) autograf
- (C) authentic
- (D) no mistake

16. The **(F)** <u>souviner</u> was quite **(G)** <u>valuable</u> to the owner, even though the real cost was **(H)** <u>inexpensive</u>. **(J)** no mistake
- (F) souviner
- (G) valuable
- (H) inexpensive
- (J) no mistake

17. In **(A)** <u>physical</u> education the **(B)** <u>instructor</u> made us try to do a **(C)** <u>summersault</u>. **(D)** no mistake
- (A) physical
- (B) instructor
- (C) summersault
- (D) no mistake

Name _____   Date _____

LANGUAGE: SPELLING
SAMPLE TEST

● **Directions:** For A, choose the word that is spelled correctly and fits best in the blank. For B, choose the phrase in which the underlined word is not spelled correctly.

Examples

A. The _____ landed just outside the city.
- (A) astroide
- (B) asturoid
- (C) asteroid
- (D) astirode

B.
- (F) manipulate the tool
- (G) bisected angle
- (H) impresive drawing
- (J) tall antenna

For numbers 1–6, find the word that is spelled correctly and fits best in the blank.

1. The _____ inventor made a startling discovery.
- (A) ambitious
- (B) ambishus
- (C) ambitus
- (D) ambichus

2. He was a _____ runner with the ball.
- (F) versatil
- (G) versatal
- (H) versatile
- (J) vursatul

3. What is the _____ policy?
- (A) cancelation
- (B) cancellation
- (C) cancelashon
- (D) cancelaton

4. The _____ was visible in the western sky.
- (F) constelation
- (G) constellation
- (H) constullation
- (J) constilation

5. She is _____ to her parents.
- (A) indeted
- (B) endeted
- (C) endebted
- (D) indebted

6. The pain was _____.
- (F) excrusiating
- (G) excrushiating
- (H) excrucieting
- (J) excruciating

For numbers 7–9, read the phrases. Choose the phrase in which the underlined word is not spelled correctly.

7.
- (A) discontinued color
- (B) spontaneous combustion
- (C) receptshonist at the desk
- (D) immense building

8.
- (F) incredible journey
- (G) initiate the action
- (H) prosperus engineer
- (J) impatient child

9.
- (A) iliterate student
- (B) gnaw on the bone
- (C) quietest of them all
- (D) latent hostility

GO ON

1-57768-978-X *Spectrum Test Practice 8*

LANGUAGE: SPELLING
SAMPLE TEST (cont.)

For numbers 10–12, read each answer. Fill in the space for the choice that has a spelling error. If there is no mistake, fill in the last answer space.

10.
- (F) calves
- (G) sheaves
- (H) heroes
- (J) no mistakes

11.
- (A) dispense
- (B) proceded
- (C) tyrant
- (D) no mistakes

12.
- (F) accidentaly
- (G) inescapable
- (H) concede
- (J) no mistakes

For numbers 13–15, read each phrase. One of the underlined words is not spelled correctly for the way it is used. Fill in the space for the word that is <u>not</u> spelled correctly.

13.
- (A) <u>immerse</u> in water
- (B) <u>impartial</u> jury
- (C) <u>inconclusive</u> results
- (D) <u>nuetral</u> position

14.
- (F) <u>ninety</u> two
- (G) <u>optamism</u> class
- (H) recent <u>occurrence</u>
- (J) <u>orchestrate</u> the action

15.
- (A) apartment <u>complex</u>
- (B) hungry and <u>penniless</u>
- (C) setting a <u>presedent</u>
- (D) <u>perpetual</u> motion

For numbers 16–19, find the underlined part that is misspelled. If all the words are spelled correctly, mark the space <u>no mistake</u>.

16. Two **(F)** <u>shipments</u> of televisions were **(G)** <u>physically</u> damaged by **(H)** <u>vandels</u>. **(J)** no mistake
- (F) shipments
- (G) physically
- (H) vandels
- (J) no mistake

17. Farmers cannot **(A)** <u>cultavate</u> their fields because of the **(B)** <u>recent</u> **(C)** <u>torrential</u> downpour. **(D)** no mistake
- (A) cultavate
- (B) recent
- (C) torrential
- (D) no mistake

18. A **(F)** <u>horrible</u> **(G)** <u>accident</u> just **(H)** <u>occurred</u> on the freeway. **(J)** no mistake
- (F) horrible
- (G) accident
- (H) occurred
- (J) no mistake

19. The **(A)** <u>personality</u> of our new **(B)** <u>secretary</u> is **(C)** <u>charming</u>. **(D)** no mistake
- (A) personality
- (B) secretary
- (C) charming
- (D) no mistake

LANGUAGE: STUDY SKILLS

● Lesson 7: Study Skills

Directions: Follow the directions for each section. Choose the answer you think is correct.

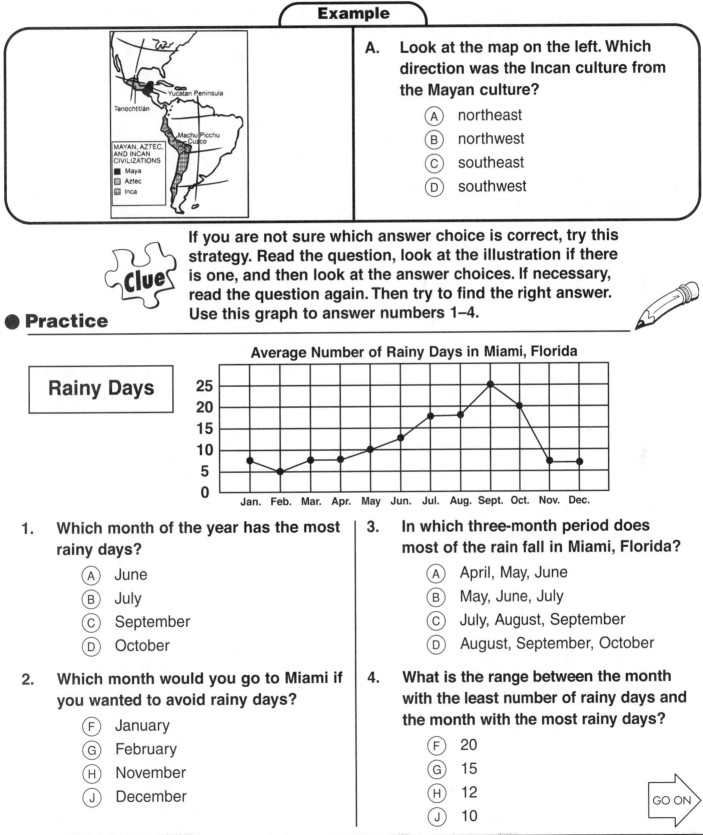

Example

A. Look at the map on the left. Which direction was the Incan culture from the Mayan culture?

- (A) northeast
- (B) northwest
- (C) southeast
- (D) southwest

Clue

If you are not sure which answer choice is correct, try this strategy. Read the question, look at the illustration if there is one, and then look at the answer choices. If necessary, read the question again. Then try to find the right answer. Use this graph to answer numbers 1–4.

● Practice

Rainy Days

Average Number of Rainy Days in Miami, Florida

1. Which month of the year has the most rainy days?
   - (A) June
   - (B) July
   - (C) September
   - (D) October

2. Which month would you go to Miami if you wanted to avoid rainy days?
   - (F) January
   - (G) February
   - (H) November
   - (J) December

3. In which three-month period does most of the rain fall in Miami, Florida?
   - (A) April, May, June
   - (B) May, June, July
   - (C) July, August, September
   - (D) August, September, October

4. What is the range between the month with the least number of rainy days and the month with the most rainy days?
   - (F) 20
   - (G) 15
   - (H) 12
   - (J) 10

GO ON

LANGUAGE: STUDY SKILLS

● Lesson 7: Study Skills (cont.)

Use the table to answer questions 5–10.

Cost of Making Money	
Denomination	Cost
$1 bill	3 cents
Half-dollar	7.8 cents
Quarter	3.7 cents
Dime	1.7 cents
Nickel	2.9 cents
Penny	0.8 cents

5. **Which denomination costs the least to make?**

   (A) penny

   (B) nickel

   (C) dime

   (D) $1 bill

6. **Which denomination is the most expensive to produce?**

   (F) quarter

   (G) half-dollar

   (H) dollar bill

   (J) nickel

7. **A nickel weighs approximately 5 grams. Which is closest to the cost per gram of making a nickel?**

   (A) slightly less than a penny

   (B) slightly more than a penny

   (C) slightly more than a half-cent

   (D) slightly less than a half-cent

8. **The average life of a $1.00 bill is 18 months. How many years does it take for the replacement cost to equal the value of $1?**

   (F) approximately 10 years

   (G) approximately 20 years

   (H) approximately 50 years

   (J) approximately 70 years

9. **The cost of making a $1 bill is what percent of its actual value?**

   (A) 3%

   (B) 15%

   (C) 22%

   (D) 31%

10. **The cost of making a half-dollar is approximately what percent of its actual value?**

    (F) 5%

    (G) 16%

    (H) 25%

    (J) 31%

Read each question below. Mark the answer that you think is correct.

11. **Which of the following would not be a good reason to use a dictionary?**

    (A) to find the definition of a word whose meaning you are uncertain of

    (B) to find the pronunciation of a word you are uncertain of

    (C) to find a word that rhymes with a word you've already used

    (D) to find another word you might use in place of this word

12. **Which of the following is not a good rule to follow when taking notes?**

    (F) Be prepared.

    (G) Listen carefully.

    (H) Find a study buddy when class is over to compare notes.

    (J) Write as quickly as you can even if some of your writing becomes difficult to read.

GO ON

Name _____   Date_____

● Lesson 7: Study Skills (cont.)

Use the information in the graph below to help you answer questions 13–16.

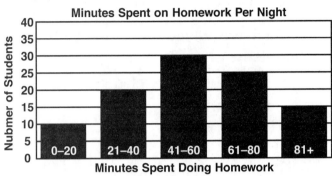

Minutes Spent on Homework Per Night

13. **If there are 100 eighth grade students, what percentage spend 20 minutes or less per night doing homework?**
    - (A) 10%
    - (B) 20%
    - (C) 30%
    - (D) 25%

14. **How many students spend more than 80 minutes per night doing homework?**
    - (F) 40
    - (G) 25
    - (H) 15
    - (J) 10

15. **How many students spend over an hour each evening doing homework?**
    - (A) 50
    - (B) 25
    - (C) 60
    - (D) 70

16. **How many students spend an hour or less each evening doing homework?**
    - (F) 60
    - (G) 40
    - (H) 30
    - (J) 25

17. **Which of the following is a good study skills rule to follow?**
    - (A) Attend class.
    - (B) Take good notes.
    - (C) Join a study group.
    - (D) All of the above are good rules to follow.

18. **Which provides the best environment in which to study?**
    - (F) at home alone in your room
    - (G) with friends outside a shopping mall
    - (H) in the living room watching television
    - (J) anywhere in the house that has the latest pop hits as background music

19. **Setting goals is a good policy in developing good study skills. Which of the following is an example of an immediate goal?**
    - (A) to get at least 85% correct on tomorrow's history test
    - (B) to gather supplies needed for my science fair project
    - (C) to get at least a B this semester in Pre-Algebra
    - (D) to become a commercial airline pilot

20. **Which of these words is not a good word to include in the vocabulary of your study skills?**
    - (F) organized
    - (G) procrastinate
    - (H) committed
    - (J) punctual

STOP

LANGUAGE: STUDY SKILLS
SAMPLE TEST

● **Directions:** Read the question. Mark the answer you think is correct.

Examples

A. Which of these would you most likely find in the index of an English book?

(A) table of contents

(B) copyright information

(C) making inferences and drawing conclusions

(D) names of authors of test

B. Which would you find in the table of contents of a magazine?

(F) subscription information

(G) credits

(H) listing of the articles and features

(J) index of advertisers

Study the table of contents from a lifestyle magazine below. Use it to do numbers 1–4.

Contents/Features

27 Special Sections
Datebook
Monthly calendar of events in the southwestern states by Jan Renard.

64 Fashionably on Course
Hit the links in style with a new look from one of the top golf outfitters.

88 Fourth Avenue Street Fair
Ben Swift points out the food fare available as well as a review of many of the wares of the street vendors and entertainment that will be available.

92 Business
Who's New/What's New? Catch-up column about new faces and places along with info on new products and services.

103 Departments
Out & About
A round-up of some of the area's best places to visit.

120 Spotlight
Previews of several of the month's major events by Barry Long

122 Destination Resorts
Executive editor Scott Hammond takes us to many of the more popular resorts in the Great Southwest, highlighting the amenities of each.

131 Dining Guide
Listing of the most popular restaurants in the Southwest as well as descriptions of the signature dinners of each.

1. Who reviews the restaurants in this month's issue?

(A) Jan Renard

(B) Barry Long

(C) Scott Hammond

(D) information is not given

2. On what page does the article begin on current golf wear?

(F) 64

(G) 88

(H) 122

(J) 145

3. On what page might you look to find out what the Fourth Avenue Street fair is all about?

(A) 64

(B) 88

(C) 122

(D) 168

4. Who has the responsibility of preparing the monthly calendar of events in the Southwest?

(F) Editor unknown

(G) Jan Renard

(H) Ben Dion

(J) Barry Swift

GO ON

Name _____   Date_____

Look at the time zones map below and answer questions 5–10.

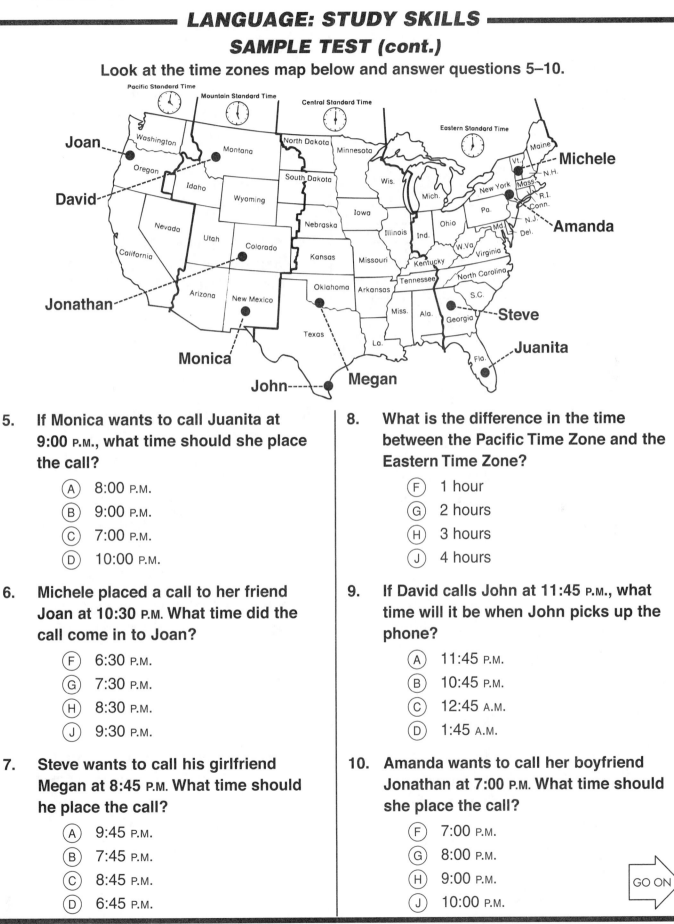

5. If Monica wants to call Juanita at 9:00 P.M., what time should she place the call?

   (A) 8:00 P.M.
   (B) 9:00 P.M.
   (C) 7:00 P.M.
   (D) 10:00 P.M.

6. Michele placed a call to her friend Joan at 10:30 P.M. What time did the call come in to Joan?

   (F) 6:30 P.M.
   (G) 7:30 P.M.
   (H) 8:30 P.M.
   (J) 9:30 P.M.

7. Steve wants to call his girlfriend Megan at 8:45 P.M. What time should he place the call?

   (A) 9:45 P.M.
   (B) 7:45 P.M.
   (C) 8:45 P.M.
   (D) 6:45 P.M.

8. What is the difference in the time between the Pacific Time Zone and the Eastern Time Zone?

   (F) 1 hour
   (G) 2 hours
   (H) 3 hours
   (J) 4 hours

9. If David calls John at 11:45 P.M., what time will it be when John picks up the phone?

   (A) 11:45 P.M.
   (B) 10:45 P.M.
   (C) 12:45 A.M.
   (D) 1:45 A.M.

10. Amanda wants to call her boyfriend Jonathan at 7:00 P.M. What time should she place the call?

   (F) 7:00 P.M.
   (G) 8:00 P.M.
   (H) 9:00 P.M.
   (J) 10:00 P.M.

GO ON

LANGUAGE: STUDY SKILLS
SAMPLE TEST (cont.)

Look at the postal rate changes table below (from the year 2001) to help you correctly answer items 11–15.

Postal Rate Change (1st ounce)

July 6, 1932	3 cents
August 1, 1958	4 cents
January 7, 1963	5 cents
January 7, 1968	6 cents
May 16, 1971	8 cents
March 2, 1974	10 cents
December 31, 1975	13 cents
May 29, 1978	15 cents
March 22, 1981	18 cents
November 1, 1981	20 cents
February 17, 1985	22 cents
April 3, 1988	25 cents
February 3, 1991	29 cents
January 1, 1995	32 cents
January 10, 1999	33 cents
January 1, 2001	34 cents

11. **Which of the following is the standard on which postal rates are based?**
    - (A) 1 ounce
    - (B) 1 pound
    - (C) 1 kilogram
    - (D) unknown

12. **Which of these years represents the least expensive rate increases?**
    - (F) 1975
    - (G) 1985
    - (H) 1999
    - (J) 1991

13. **Which of these years represents the largest increase in postal rates?**
    - (A) 1958
    - (B) 1975
    - (C) 1991
    - (D) 2001

14. **How many postal increases have occurred in taking us from a rate of 3 cents to the rate of 34 cents?**
    - (F) 12
    - (G) 13
    - (H) 14
    - (J) 15

15. **How many times has the U.S. Postal Service raised the postal rate just one cent between 1932 and 2001?**
    - (A) none
    - (B) 4
    - (C) 5
    - (D) 6

16. **Setting goals is a great way to develop better study skills. Which of the following is an example of a long range goal?**
    - (F) Getting through this year
    - (G) Getting through tomorrow's test
    - (H) Becoming a doctor someday
    - (J) Making dinner tonight

17. **Which of the following would be the best source for finding the synonym of a word?**
    - (A) dictionary
    - (B) encyclopedia
    - (C) thesaurus
    - (D) almanac

18. **Which of these sources provides the most recent information on a current topic?**
    - (F) encyclopedia
    - (G) Internet
    - (H) yearbook
    - (J) almanac

ANSWER SHEET

STUDENT'S NAME			SCHOOL
LAST	FIRST	MI	TEACHER

FEMALE ◯　　　　MALE ◯

Ⓐ Ⓐ Ⓐ Ⓐ Ⓐ Ⓐ Ⓐ Ⓐ Ⓐ Ⓐ Ⓐ　Ⓐ Ⓐ Ⓐ Ⓐ Ⓐ Ⓐ Ⓐ　Ⓐ
Ⓑ Ⓑ Ⓑ Ⓑ Ⓑ Ⓑ Ⓑ Ⓑ Ⓑ Ⓑ Ⓑ　Ⓑ Ⓑ Ⓑ Ⓑ Ⓑ Ⓑ Ⓑ　Ⓑ
Ⓒ Ⓒ Ⓒ Ⓒ Ⓒ Ⓒ Ⓒ Ⓒ Ⓒ Ⓒ Ⓒ　Ⓒ Ⓒ Ⓒ Ⓒ Ⓒ Ⓒ Ⓒ　Ⓒ
Ⓓ Ⓓ Ⓓ Ⓓ Ⓓ Ⓓ Ⓓ Ⓓ Ⓓ Ⓓ Ⓓ　Ⓓ Ⓓ Ⓓ Ⓓ Ⓓ Ⓓ Ⓓ　Ⓓ
Ⓔ Ⓔ Ⓔ Ⓔ Ⓔ Ⓔ Ⓔ Ⓔ Ⓔ Ⓔ Ⓔ　Ⓔ Ⓔ Ⓔ Ⓔ Ⓔ Ⓔ Ⓔ　Ⓔ
Ⓕ Ⓕ Ⓕ Ⓕ Ⓕ Ⓕ Ⓕ Ⓕ Ⓕ Ⓕ Ⓕ　Ⓕ Ⓕ Ⓕ Ⓕ Ⓕ Ⓕ Ⓕ　Ⓕ
Ⓖ Ⓖ Ⓖ Ⓖ Ⓖ Ⓖ Ⓖ Ⓖ Ⓖ Ⓖ Ⓖ　Ⓖ Ⓖ Ⓖ Ⓖ Ⓖ Ⓖ Ⓖ　Ⓖ
Ⓗ Ⓗ Ⓗ Ⓗ Ⓗ Ⓗ Ⓗ Ⓗ Ⓗ Ⓗ Ⓗ　Ⓗ Ⓗ Ⓗ Ⓗ Ⓗ Ⓗ Ⓗ　Ⓗ
Ⓘ Ⓘ Ⓘ Ⓘ Ⓘ Ⓘ Ⓘ Ⓘ Ⓘ Ⓘ Ⓘ　Ⓘ Ⓘ Ⓘ Ⓘ Ⓘ Ⓘ Ⓘ　Ⓘ
Ⓙ Ⓙ Ⓙ Ⓙ Ⓙ Ⓙ Ⓙ Ⓙ Ⓙ Ⓙ Ⓙ　Ⓙ Ⓙ Ⓙ Ⓙ Ⓙ Ⓙ Ⓙ　Ⓙ
Ⓚ Ⓚ Ⓚ Ⓚ Ⓚ Ⓚ Ⓚ Ⓚ Ⓚ Ⓚ Ⓚ　Ⓚ Ⓚ Ⓚ Ⓚ Ⓚ Ⓚ Ⓚ　Ⓚ
Ⓛ Ⓛ Ⓛ Ⓛ Ⓛ Ⓛ Ⓛ Ⓛ Ⓛ Ⓛ Ⓛ　Ⓛ Ⓛ Ⓛ Ⓛ Ⓛ Ⓛ Ⓛ　Ⓛ
Ⓜ Ⓜ Ⓜ Ⓜ Ⓜ Ⓜ Ⓜ Ⓜ Ⓜ Ⓜ Ⓜ　Ⓜ Ⓜ Ⓜ Ⓜ Ⓜ Ⓜ Ⓜ　Ⓜ
Ⓝ Ⓝ Ⓝ Ⓝ Ⓝ Ⓝ Ⓝ Ⓝ Ⓝ Ⓝ Ⓝ　Ⓝ Ⓝ Ⓝ Ⓝ Ⓝ Ⓝ Ⓝ　Ⓝ
Ⓞ Ⓞ Ⓞ Ⓞ Ⓞ Ⓞ Ⓞ Ⓞ Ⓞ Ⓞ Ⓞ　Ⓞ Ⓞ Ⓞ Ⓞ Ⓞ Ⓞ Ⓞ　Ⓞ
Ⓟ Ⓟ Ⓟ Ⓟ Ⓟ Ⓟ Ⓟ Ⓟ Ⓟ Ⓟ Ⓟ　Ⓟ Ⓟ Ⓟ Ⓟ Ⓟ Ⓟ Ⓟ　Ⓟ
Ⓠ Ⓠ Ⓠ Ⓠ Ⓠ Ⓠ Ⓠ Ⓠ Ⓠ Ⓠ Ⓠ　Ⓠ Ⓠ Ⓠ Ⓠ Ⓠ Ⓠ Ⓠ　Ⓠ
Ⓡ Ⓡ Ⓡ Ⓡ Ⓡ Ⓡ Ⓡ Ⓡ Ⓡ Ⓡ Ⓡ　Ⓡ Ⓡ Ⓡ Ⓡ Ⓡ Ⓡ Ⓡ　Ⓡ
Ⓢ Ⓢ Ⓢ Ⓢ Ⓢ Ⓢ Ⓢ Ⓢ Ⓢ Ⓢ Ⓢ　Ⓢ Ⓢ Ⓢ Ⓢ Ⓢ Ⓢ Ⓢ　Ⓢ
Ⓣ Ⓣ Ⓣ Ⓣ Ⓣ Ⓣ Ⓣ Ⓣ Ⓣ Ⓣ Ⓣ　Ⓣ Ⓣ Ⓣ Ⓣ Ⓣ Ⓣ Ⓣ　Ⓣ
Ⓤ Ⓤ Ⓤ Ⓤ Ⓤ Ⓤ Ⓤ Ⓤ Ⓤ Ⓤ Ⓤ　Ⓤ Ⓤ Ⓤ Ⓤ Ⓤ Ⓤ Ⓤ　Ⓤ
Ⓥ Ⓥ Ⓥ Ⓥ Ⓥ Ⓥ Ⓥ Ⓥ Ⓥ Ⓥ Ⓥ　Ⓥ Ⓥ Ⓥ Ⓥ Ⓥ Ⓥ Ⓥ　Ⓥ
Ⓦ Ⓦ Ⓦ Ⓦ Ⓦ Ⓦ Ⓦ Ⓦ Ⓦ Ⓦ Ⓦ　Ⓦ Ⓦ Ⓦ Ⓦ Ⓦ Ⓦ Ⓦ　Ⓦ
Ⓧ Ⓧ Ⓧ Ⓧ Ⓧ Ⓧ Ⓧ Ⓧ Ⓧ Ⓧ Ⓧ　Ⓧ Ⓧ Ⓧ Ⓧ Ⓧ Ⓧ Ⓧ　Ⓧ
Ⓨ Ⓨ Ⓨ Ⓨ Ⓨ Ⓨ Ⓨ Ⓨ Ⓨ Ⓨ Ⓨ　Ⓨ Ⓨ Ⓨ Ⓨ Ⓨ Ⓨ Ⓨ　Ⓨ
Ⓩ Ⓩ Ⓩ Ⓩ Ⓩ Ⓩ Ⓩ Ⓩ Ⓩ Ⓩ Ⓩ　Ⓩ Ⓩ Ⓩ Ⓩ Ⓩ Ⓩ Ⓩ　Ⓩ

BIRTH DATE

MONTH	DAY	YEAR
JAN ◯	⓪ ⓪	⓪
FEB ◯	① ①	①
MAR ◯	② ②	②
APR ◯	③ ③	③
MAY ◯	④	④
JUN ◯	⑤	⑤ ⑤
JUL ◯	⑥	⑥ ⑥
AUG ◯	⑦	⑦ ⑦
SEP ◯	⑧	⑧ ⑧
OCT ◯	⑨	⑨ ⑨
NOV ◯	⓪	
DEC ◯		

GRADE
⑦　⑧　⑨

Part 1: MECHANICS

A Ⓐ Ⓑ Ⓒ Ⓓ	4 Ⓕ Ⓖ Ⓗ Ⓙ	8 Ⓕ Ⓖ Ⓗ Ⓙ	12 Ⓕ Ⓖ Ⓗ Ⓙ	16 Ⓕ Ⓖ Ⓗ Ⓙ	20 Ⓕ Ⓖ Ⓗ Ⓙ
1 Ⓐ Ⓑ Ⓒ Ⓓ	5 Ⓐ Ⓑ Ⓒ Ⓓ	9 Ⓐ Ⓑ Ⓒ Ⓓ	13 Ⓐ Ⓑ Ⓒ Ⓓ	17 Ⓐ Ⓑ Ⓒ Ⓓ	21 Ⓐ Ⓑ Ⓒ Ⓓ
2 Ⓕ Ⓖ Ⓗ Ⓙ	6 Ⓕ Ⓖ Ⓗ Ⓙ	10 Ⓕ Ⓖ Ⓗ Ⓙ	14 Ⓕ Ⓖ Ⓗ Ⓙ	18 Ⓕ Ⓖ Ⓗ Ⓙ	
3 Ⓐ Ⓑ Ⓒ Ⓓ	7 Ⓐ Ⓑ Ⓒ Ⓓ	11 Ⓐ Ⓑ Ⓒ Ⓓ	15 Ⓐ Ⓑ Ⓒ Ⓓ	19 Ⓐ Ⓑ Ⓒ Ⓓ	

Part 2: EXPRESSION

A Ⓐ Ⓑ Ⓒ Ⓓ	3 Ⓐ Ⓑ Ⓒ Ⓓ	6 Ⓕ Ⓖ Ⓗ Ⓙ	9 Ⓐ Ⓑ Ⓒ Ⓓ	12 Ⓕ Ⓖ Ⓗ Ⓙ	15 Ⓐ Ⓑ Ⓒ Ⓓ
1 Ⓐ Ⓑ Ⓒ Ⓓ	4 Ⓕ Ⓖ Ⓗ Ⓙ	7 Ⓐ Ⓑ Ⓒ Ⓓ	10 Ⓕ Ⓖ Ⓗ Ⓙ	13 Ⓐ Ⓑ Ⓒ Ⓓ	16 Ⓕ Ⓖ Ⓗ Ⓙ
2 Ⓕ Ⓖ Ⓗ Ⓙ	5 Ⓐ Ⓑ Ⓒ Ⓓ	8 Ⓕ Ⓖ Ⓗ Ⓙ	11 Ⓐ Ⓑ Ⓒ Ⓓ	14 Ⓕ Ⓖ Ⓗ Ⓙ	

Part 3: SPELLING

A Ⓐ Ⓑ Ⓒ Ⓓ	3 Ⓐ Ⓑ Ⓒ Ⓓ	7 Ⓐ Ⓑ Ⓒ Ⓓ	11 Ⓐ Ⓑ Ⓒ Ⓓ	15 Ⓐ Ⓑ Ⓒ Ⓓ	19 Ⓐ Ⓑ Ⓒ Ⓓ
B Ⓕ Ⓖ Ⓗ Ⓙ	4 Ⓕ Ⓖ Ⓗ Ⓙ	8 Ⓕ Ⓖ Ⓗ Ⓙ	12 Ⓕ Ⓖ Ⓗ Ⓙ	16 Ⓕ Ⓖ Ⓗ Ⓙ	
1 Ⓐ Ⓑ Ⓒ Ⓓ	5 Ⓐ Ⓑ Ⓒ Ⓓ	9 Ⓐ Ⓑ Ⓒ Ⓓ	13 Ⓐ Ⓑ Ⓒ Ⓓ	17 Ⓐ Ⓑ Ⓒ Ⓓ	
2 Ⓕ Ⓖ Ⓗ Ⓙ	6 Ⓕ Ⓖ Ⓗ Ⓙ	10 Ⓕ Ⓖ Ⓗ Ⓙ	14 Ⓕ Ⓖ Ⓗ Ⓙ	18 Ⓕ Ⓖ Ⓗ Ⓙ	

Part 4: STUDY SKILLS

A Ⓐ Ⓑ Ⓒ Ⓓ	2 Ⓕ Ⓖ Ⓗ Ⓙ	4 Ⓕ Ⓖ Ⓗ Ⓙ	6 Ⓕ Ⓖ Ⓗ Ⓙ	8 Ⓕ Ⓖ Ⓗ Ⓙ	10 Ⓕ Ⓖ Ⓗ Ⓙ
1 Ⓐ Ⓑ Ⓒ Ⓓ	3 Ⓐ Ⓑ Ⓒ Ⓓ	5 Ⓐ Ⓑ Ⓒ Ⓓ	7 Ⓐ Ⓑ Ⓒ Ⓓ	9 Ⓐ Ⓑ Ⓒ Ⓓ	

LANGUAGE: PRACTICE TEST

● Part 1: Mechanics

Directions: Fill in the answer choice for the punctuation mark that is needed. Choose "none" if no more punctuation is needed in the sentence.

Example

A. Did Tom remove his cap when he came in

   (A) ;

   (B) .

   (C) ?

   (D) none

1. When you go to the beach you should remember to take sunscreen along.

   (A) :

   (B) ;

   (C) ,

   (D) none

2. The basketball team returned to their home city and were greeted by thousands of cheering fans.

   (F) ;

   (G) :

   (H) ,

   (J) none

3. How will you ever get that stain out of your shirt

   (A) ,

   (B) ?

   (C) ;

   (D) none

4. Uncle Fred my favorite uncle, came to our house for Thanksgiving dinner.

   (F) :

   (G) ,

   (H) !

   (J) none

For numbers 5–7, read each answer. Fill in the space for the choice that has a punctuation error. If there is no mistake, fill in the fourth answer space.

5. (A) Holmes leaned forward and tried

   (B) to contain his excitement but

   (C) his look gave away his feelings.

   (D) no mistakes

6. (F) I like many foods, but

   (G) these are my favorites

   (H) pizza, ice cream, and cheeseburgers.

   (J) no mistakes

7. (A) Mr. Bentley assembled the

   (B) entire student body outside

   (C) the school for a drill.

   (D) no mistakes

For numbers 8 and 9, read each sentence. Choose the word or words that fit best in the blank and show correct punctuation.

8. The software will be delivered to you by _____ shipping costs will be free.

   (F) Friday. Or

   (G) Tuesday: or

   (H) Friday, or

   (J) Friday or,

GO ON

LANGUAGE: PRACTICE TEST
Part 1: Mechanics (cont.)

9. There were six young colts in the meadow besides _____ were older than I was.

   (A) me, they
   (B) me? They
   (C) me; they
   (D) me: they

For numbers 10–12, read each answer. Fill in the space for the choice that has a capitalization error. If there is no mistake, fill in the fourth answer space.

10. (F) Those tournaments are the PGA,
     (G) the masters, the U.S. Open, and
     (H) the British Open.
     (J) no mistakes

11. (A) On that date, Cal Ripkin, Jr.
     (B) broke Lou Gehrig's record of
     (C) 2,130 consecutive games.
     (D) no mistakes

12. (F) Arthur Ashe was the first black
     (G) male to reach the final match
     (H) at wimbleton.
     (J) no mistakes

For number 13, read each group of sentences. Find the one that is written correctly and shows correct capitalization and punctuation.

13. (A) Hundreds of golfers try each year to qualify for the professional tour. Qualifying tournaments are held throughout the nation. In the tournament finals, only 25 cards are issued.
     (B) "I don't know anything about children" said Mr. Craven. "I sent for you today because Mrs. Sowerby said I ought to see you.
     (C) Annie said, "I knew a girl in

Marysville who could walk the ridgepole of a roof." "Don't you try it, Annie!" yelled Diana. You will fall and hurt yourself badly."

   (D) The rules and regulations of volleyball are fairly easy to understand. A point or Side Out is awarded for each service. A well played Volleyball game is entertaining to watch.

For numbers 14–16, read the sentence with a blank. Mark the space beside the answer choice that fits best in the blank and has correct capitalization and punctuation.

14. The coach of the golf team, _____ gives golf balls to all members of the team before each match.

   (F) Ross Bennet
   (G) Ross Bennet:
   (H) Ross Bennet;
   (J) Ross Bennet,

15. The tallest peak I can see from my house is _____ It is more than 9000 feet high.

   (A) mt. Lemmon
   (B) Mt. Lemmon;
   (C) Mt. Lemmon.
   (D) Mt. Lemmon,

16. The street fair opens on _____ I can't go until Saturday.

   (F) Friday but
   (G) Friday. But
   (H) Friday, but
   (J) Friday: but

GO ON

LANGUAGE: PRACTICE TEST
Part 1: Mechanics (cont.)

Choose the correct answer for number 17.

17. **Which of the following is the best way to begin a friendly letter?**
    - (A) Dear Cameron,
    - (B) Dear Cameron!
    - (C) Dear Cameron:
    - (D) Dear Cameron;

Following is a letter written by Garrett from scout camp to his parents back home. Use it to complete numbers 18–21.

Dear Mom and Dad,

(1) I'm having a great time here but I still miss both of you lots! **(2)** How is the dog getting along? **(3)** I bet he's spending a lot of time by the door with his tail down. **(4)** Please give him a biscuit for me and mention my name.

(5) We're spending a lot of time swimming in the fox river but I enjoy the canoeing even more! **(6)** We're divided into teams and we're going to have canoe races on Thursday. **(7)** Our team is called the Pirates however I doubt that we will win. **(8)** Our guys really aren't very good at paddling, but we sure do have fun!

(9) The food is okay, but it isn't nearly as good as the way you cook mom. **(10)** I've learned how to pitch a tent and tie some nifty knots. **(11)** I sort of wish you were both here. I'm a little bit homesick. **(12)** I have to get ready for a hike. **(13)** Bye for now.

Love,
Garrett

18. **In sentence 1, here but is best written—**
    - (F) here: but
    - (G) here, but
    - (H) here; but
    - (J) As it is

19. **In sentence 5, the fox river but is best written—**
    - (A) The Fox River, but
    - (B) the Fox River, but
    - (C) the Fox River; but
    - (D) As it is

20. **In sentence 7, Pirates however is best written—**
    - (F) Pirates: however,
    - (G) Pirates; however,
    - (H) Pirates, however
    - (J) As it is

21. **In sentence 9, you cook mom is best written—**
    - (A) You cook, Mom.
    - (B) you cook; mom
    - (C) you cook, Mom.
    - (D) As it is.

Name _____   Date _____

LANGUAGE: PRACTICE TEST

● Part 2: Expression

Directions: Find the underlined part that is the simple predicate (verb) of the sentence.

Example

A.   In **(A)** time the **(B)** best **(C)** team **(D)** reached the top of the standings.

- Ⓐ time
- Ⓑ best
- Ⓒ team
- Ⓓ reached

For number 1, choose the word or phrase that best completes the sentence.

1.   The coyote _____ all of the dog food and the scraps of bread that were left for the birds.

- Ⓐ eating
- Ⓑ were eaten
- Ⓒ have eaten
- Ⓓ has eaten

For number 2, choose the answer that is a complete and correctly written sentence.

2.   Ⓕ If you want we can meet in front of the theater just before the movie begins

Ⓖ We can also meet at, Amy's house which is close to the theater.

Ⓗ We must decide on a plan soon; or go on to a later movie

Ⓙ If we don't decide soon, we'll miss the movie we're planning to see!

For numbers 3–5, read each answer. Fill in the space of the choice that has an error. If there is no mistake, fill in the fourth space.

3.   Ⓐ Angie's name was listed near the top

Ⓑ of the program because her last name

Ⓒ starts with the letter B.

Ⓓ no mistakes

4.   Ⓕ The Miami Dolphins were unbeaten in the

Ⓖ 1972 season: the first such team in over 30

Ⓗ years to win all of its games.

Ⓙ no mistakes

5.   Ⓐ Jose did not appreciate having

Ⓑ anyone leave fingerprints on

Ⓒ his freshly waxed car.

Ⓓ no mistakes

For number 6, find the underlined part that is the simple subject of the sentence.

6.   The **(F)** new **(G)** television doesn't seem to **(H)** work **(J)** properly.

- Ⓕ new
- Ⓖ television
- Ⓗ work
- Ⓙ properly

For number 7, find the underlined part that is the simple predicate (verb) of the sentence.

7.   **(A)** Cacti **(B)** often **(C)** grow in very unusual **(D)** places.

- Ⓐ Cacti
- Ⓑ often
- Ⓒ grow
- Ⓓ places

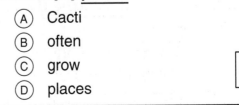
GO ON

For numbers 8–10, choose the answer that best combines the underlined sentences.

8. **My bicycle is in the shed behind our house. I'm sure it has a flat tire.**

    (F) I'm sure it has a flat tire, even though my bicycle is in the shed behind our house.

    (G) While I'm sure it has a flat tire, my bicycle is in the shed behind our house.

    (H) My bicycle is in the shed behind our house, but I'm sure it has a flat tire.

    (J) My bicycle is in the shed behind our house, even if it has a flat tire.

9. **Your friend came to our house yesterday afternoon. Your friend left his sweater in the living room.**

    (A) Your friend, who came to our house yesterday afternoon, left his sweater in the living room.

    (B) Your friend left his sweater in the living room, even though he was here yesterday.

    (C) While your friend was here yesterday, he came to our house and left his sweater.

    (D) Your friend came here and left his sweater, but he was here yesterday afternoon.

10. **Tami is Toni's sister. Tami went to the University of Illinois. The University of Illinois is in Champaign.**

    (F) The University of Illinois, which is in Champaign, which is where Tami went, who is Toni's sister.

    (G) Tami, who is Toni's sister, went to Champaign, where the University of Illinois is.

    (H) Toni's sister, Tami, went to the University of Illinois, which is in Champaign.

    (J) The University of Illinois, which is in Champaign, is where Toni's sister Tami went.

For numbers 11 and 12, choose the best way of expressing the idea.

11. (A) While you are in the mall, will you look for the things I've jotted down on this list?

    (B) On this list I have jotted down things while you are at the mall you can get for me.

    (C) At the mall are the things I've jotted down on this list, which I hope you will get for me.

    (D) Although you may go to the mall please pick up the things I've jotted down while you're there.

12. (F) If you don't pass this course, then you should probably take the same course again this summer.

    (G) Eric, this summer you should take the course again if you don't pass it in the spring.

    (H) Eric, if you don't pass this course, Eric, you should probably take it again this summer.

    (J) Eric, you should pass this course, but if you don't then you should take it again in the summer.

GO ON

Read the paragraph below. Find the best topic sentence for the paragraph.

13. _____ Carrier pigeons can fly great distances and find their way back home very accurately. Because of these navigational instincts, pigeons have been used even during wars to carry important messages.

   (A) Carrier pigeons love to engage in racing with other pigeons.

   (B) Carrier pigeons have sometimes been used to do important deeds for man.

   (C) Carrier pigeons sometimes are very dirty and people don't like them.

   (D) Large and small pigeons can travel equally fast.

Find the answer choice that best develops the topic sentence.

14. **Many people in the West are finding ways of creating gardens that require very little water.**

   (F) Lawns that require a great deal of water require even more water in dry years. Then you need to mow the grass and fertilize often.

   (G) There are many different kinds of cacti. They make wonderful outdoor plants and are great in gardens.

   (H) Since it's hot and dry in the desert, plants that do well in the East don't do very well in this climate.

   (J) Gardening that makes use of native plants that thrive in a dry climate can be both fun and attractive if designed properly.

Read the paragraph below. Find the sentence that does not belong in the paragraph.

15. **(1)** The names Ben Franklin, George Washington, and Patrick Henry have long been associated with the American Revolution. **(2)** But there were also many women who helped in the cause for freedom of the colonies. **(3)** Molly Pitcher was one of those women. **(4)** While her name sounds funny, you may know her real name.

   (A) Sentence 1

   (B) Sentence 2

   (C) Sentence 3

   (D) Sentence 4

Read the paragraph below. Find the sentence that best fits the blank in the paragraph.

16. **The federal government pays for many of the services we enjoy and other programs that are of benefit to many of us. _____ Then the president prepares a budget that shows how much money will be needed for the coming year. Congress then votes on the budget and makes final decisions on how the money will be spent.**

   (F) The president looks at the current budget and tries to raise it as much as he can.

   (G) The president tries to determine how much income the government will be receiving from taxes.

   (H) Congress never approves the president's budget the first time.

   (J) Taxes are only raised if the budget requires them to be raised.

STOP

85

LANGUAGE: PRACTICE TEST

● Part 3: Spelling

Directions: For A, find the word that is spelled correctly and fits best in the blank. For B, choose the phrase in which the underlined word is not spelled correctly.

Examples

A. What did the company _____ to you?
- (A) reccomend
- (B) reccommend
- (C) recommend
- (D) recomend

B.
- (F) gas recipt
- (G) proper pronoun
- (H) impartial jury
- (J) preview of the movie

For numbers 1–5, find the word that is spelled correctly and fits best in the blank.

1. He was a _____ citizen.
   - (A) prominent
   - (B) prominant
   - (C) promenent
   - (D) promienant

2. The clock was set into _____ motion.
   - (F) prepetal
   - (G) perputual
   - (H) perpetual
   - (J) peretull

3. I have been asked to _____ the test.
   - (A) monitiore
   - (B) monitur
   - (C) monitor
   - (D) monetor

4. The lights _____ the tree.
   - (F) ilumminate
   - (G) illuminate
   - (H) eluminate
   - (J) illuminat

5. It should be an _____ journey.
   - (A) inncredible
   - (B) incredable
   - (C) incredbal
   - (D) incredible

For numbers 6–9, read the phrases. Choose the phrase in which the underlined word is not spelled correctly.

6.
- (F) the freedom trail
- (G) in all honesty
- (H) irregulare shape
- (J) launch the year

7.
- (A) leizure time
- (B) sleepy lagoon
- (C) Greek mythology
- (D) satellite service

8.
- (F) fresh samon
- (G) animal scent
- (H) difficult schedule
- (J) steady diet

9.
- (A) shrewd deal
- (B) holiday occasions
- (C) rare opportunity
- (D) nateral foods

GO ON

For numbers 10–12, read each answer. Fill in the space for the choice that has a spelling error. If there is no mistake, fill in the last answer space.

10.
- (F) invention
- (G) invasion
- (H) physican
- (J) no mistakes

11.
- (A) thief
- (B) neither
- (C) leisure
- (D) no mistakes

12.
- (F) mischief
- (G) weird
- (H) heighth
- (J) no mistakes

For numbers 13–15, read each phrase. One of the underlined words is not spelled correctly for the way it is used in the phrase. Fill in the space for the word that is not spelled correctly.

13.
- (A) <u>beige</u> color
- (B) good <u>hygiene</u>
- (C) <u>sealing</u> fan
- (D) <u>excellent</u> grade

14.
- (F) <u>grate</u> golfer
- (G) court <u>brief</u>
- (H) yours <u>truly</u>
- (J) <u>succeed</u> in life

15.
- (A) <u>immature</u> boy
- (B) monthly <u>meetting</u>
- (C) <u>controllable</u> issue
- (D) <u>donkey</u> basketball

For numbers 16–19, find the underlined part that is misspelled. If all words are spelled correctly, mark the space for no mistakes.

16. Courtney's **(F)** <u>opinion</u> was not in **(G)** <u>accord</u> with the **(H)** <u>assembly</u>. **(J)** no mistake
- (F) opinion
- (G) accord
- (H) assembly
- (J) no mistakes

17. The **(A)** <u>legend</u> of the **(B)** <u>beligerent</u> student was **(C)** <u>inaccurate</u>. **(D)** no mistake
- (A) legend
- (B) beligerent
- (C) inaccurate
- (D) no mistakes

18. The **(F)** <u>kitchen</u> **(G)** <u>cabinet</u> came down **(H)** <u>unexpectedly</u>. **(J)** no mistake
- (F) kitchen
- (G) cabinet
- (H) unexpectedly
- (J) no mistakes

19. **(A)** <u>Neither</u> my **(B)** <u>neice</u> nor my **(C)** <u>nephew</u> wanted dinner. **(D)** no mistake
- (A) neither
- (B) neice
- (C) nephew
- (D) no mistakes

LANGUAGE: PRACTICE TEST

● Part 4: Study Skills

Directions: Study the outline. Then choose the answer you think is correct.

Example

A.   **Outline**
    Winter Sports
    1. Skiing
    2. Snowboarding
    3. Ski Jumping
    4. _____
    5. Ice hockey
	Which of these would fit best in Line 4 of the outline on the left?
	    Ⓐ Bowling
	    Ⓑ Racquetball
	    Ⓒ Curling
	    Ⓓ Roller Blading

Study the map on the right that charts the journey of Meriwether Lewis and William Clark as they explored the vast land known as Louisiana. Use the map to do numbers 1–4.

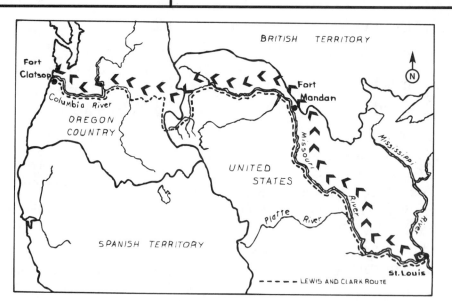

1. **The journey of Lewis and Clark was launched at _____.**
    Ⓐ Fort Mandan
    Ⓑ Fort Clatsop
    Ⓒ St. Louis
    Ⓓ unknown

2. **The river used by Lewis and Clark during the first part of their journey was the _____ River.**
    Ⓕ Mississippi
    Ⓖ Platte
    Ⓗ Missouri
    Ⓙ Columbia

3. **The direction in which the Lewis and Clark journey began was _____.**
    Ⓐ northeast
    Ⓑ northwest
    Ⓒ southwest
    Ⓓ southeast

4. **The final leg of their journey in reaching the Pacific Ocean was their trip down the _____ River.**
    Ⓕ Mississippi
    Ⓖ Platte
    Ⓗ Missouri
    Ⓙ Columbia

GO ON

Look at the guide words below that appear on a page in a dictionary. Which of these words would be on that page?

5. **marjoram-maroon**
   - (A) monsoon
   - (B) marsupial
   - (C) marmot
   - (D) marquee

Look at the guide words below from this dictionary page. Which of these words would be found on that page?

6. **draw-dredging**
   - (F) driftwood
   - (G) drape
   - (H) dream
   - (J) driver

7. Which of these is a main heading that includes the other three words?
   - (A) cats
   - (B) tigers
   - (C) mammals
   - (D) dogs

8. Which of these might be found in a book chapter entitled "Unusual Hobbies?"
   - (F) collecting marbles
   - (G) collecting baseball cards
   - (H) collecting stamps
   - (J) collecting salad forks

Here is a map that Jeff drew to show his friends how to get from Huntsville to the observatory. Use the map to do numbers 9 and 10.

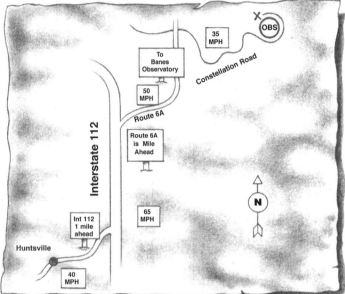

9. When people are following Jeff's map, which road are they on when they see a sign directing them to their destination?
   - (A) Huntsdale Road
   - (B) Interstate 112
   - (C) Route 6A
   - (D) Constellation Road

10. According to your answer for number 9, how fast will they be driving before they make the turn toward their destination?
    - (F) 40 miles per hour
    - (G) 65 miles per hour
    - (H) 50 miles per hour
    - (J) 35 miles per hour

MATH: CONCEPTS

● Lesson 1: Numeration

Directions: Read and work each problem. Find the correct answer. Fill in the circle that corresponds with your choice.

Examples

A. Which of these numbers comes between 86 and 110?

- (A) 130
- (B) 98
- (C) 79
- (D) 128

B. In which of these problems can the dividend be evenly divided by the divisor?

- (F) $125 \div 9$
- (G) $122 \div 8$
- (H) $126 \div 8$
- (J) $126 \div 9$

Clue Read each question carefully. Look for key words and numbers that will help you find the answers. Look at each answer choice before you choose the one you think is correct.

● Practice

1. To which value does Arrow D point?

- (A) $1\frac{1}{4}$
- (B) $\frac{1}{2}$
- (C) $^-1\frac{1}{4}$
- (D) $^-2\frac{1}{4}$

2. What number should replace the _____ to make the following a true statement?

$$763,812 = \underline{\hspace{1cm}} + 60,000 + 3,000 + 800 + 10 + 2$$

- (F) 700,000
- (G) 7,000,000
- (H) 700
- (J) 70,000

3. Another way to write 4^5 is

- (A) $4 + 5$
- (B) 4×5
- (C) $5 \times 5 \times 5 \times 5$
- (D) $4 \times 4 \times 4 \times 4 \times 4$

4. What number is 30,000 more than 25,972,043?

- (F) 25,942,043
- (G) 26,002,043
- (H) 26,012,043
- (J) 26,112,043

5. What is the greatest common factor of 52 and 156?

- (A) 84
- (B) 52
- (C) 9
- (D) 90

GO ON

MATH: CONCEPTS

● Lesson 1: Numeration (cont.)

6. Which of the number sentences below is <u>false</u>?
   - (F) $^-3 < 1$
   - (G) $5 < {}^-2$
   - (H) $3 > {}^-3$
   - (J) $^-5 > {}^-6$

7. What is the value of the expression below?

   $$(6 + 4)^2 \div 5$$

   - (A) 14
   - (B) 10
   - (C) 18
   - (D) 20

8. The value of $\sqrt{39}$ is between
   - (F) 5 and 6
   - (G) 6 and 7
   - (H) 7 and 8
   - (J) 3 and 5

9. What is the <u>least</u> number that is divisible by <u>27 and 81</u>?
   - (A) 54
   - (B) 81
   - (C) 243
   - (D) 486

10. What is the prime factorization of 72?
    - (F) $2 \times 2 \times 2 \times 3 \times 3$
    - (G) $2 \times 3 \times 2 \times 3$
    - (H) 6×12
    - (J) 9×8

11. $6.12 \times 10^5 =$
    - (A) 60,210
    - (B) 612
    - (C) 6,120,000
    - (D) 612,000

12. Which number is between $^-8$ and 8?
    - (F) $^-3$
    - (G) $^-9$
    - (H) $^-15$
    - (J) 9

13. Which group of integers is in order from greatest to least?
    - (A) $^-3, {}^-2, 0, 2, 5$
    - (B) $9, 7, 2, 0, {}^-3$
    - (C) $^-8, {}^-5, 0, 10, 13$
    - (D) $^-9, {}^-5, {}^-1, 0, 6$

14. Which of these statements is true?
    - (F) $a - b = b - a$
    - (G) $a + b = b \div a$
    - (H) $a + b = b + a$
    - (J) $a + b = b \times a$

15. For graduation, students were seated in rows of 37 each except for the last row which had only 13 students. Which of the following answers could represent the number of students graduating?
    - (A) 186
    - (B) 309
    - (C) 79
    - (D) 404

GO ON

MATH: CONCEPTS

● Lesson 1: Numeration (cont.)

16. **What is the prime factorization of 98?**

    - (F) 2 x 2 x 2 x 7
    - (G) 2 x 7 x 7 x 7
    - (H) 2 x 7 x 7
    - (J) 3 x 32

17. **Which of these sentences is true?**

    - (A) 5 > 8
    - (B) ⁻2 < ⁻9
    - (C) ⁻2 > ⁻4
    - (D) ⁻4 < ⁻8

18. **Which is another way to write 5 x 5 x 5 x 5?**

    - (F) 5^3
    - (G) 5^4
    - (H) 5^5
    - (J) 25^5

19. **Which group of integers is in order from least to greatest?**

    - (A) 0, 2, 4, ⁻5, 6
    - (B) ⁻2, ⁻1, 0, 2, 4
    - (C) 4, 2, 0, ⁻1, ⁻2
    - (D) ⁻5, ⁻6, ⁻8, ⁻9, ⁻10

20. **What number should replace the blank space to make the following a true statement?**

    1,064,018 = _____ + 60,000 + 4,000 + 10 + 8

    - (F) 64,000
    - (G) 100,000
    - (H) 1,000,000
    - (J) 10,000

21. **Which of these is not a factor of 2,478?**

    - (A) 7
    - (B) 42
    - (C) 32
    - (D) 59

22. **What number is 25,000 less than 28,372,896?**

    - (F) 28,473,086
    - (G) 28,347,896
    - (H) 28,474,086
    - (J) 28,273,896

23. **Solve $\sqrt{196}$**

    - (A) 11
    - (B) 13
    - (C) 14
    - (D) 17

24. **Which number is between ⁻9 and ⁻15?**

    - (F) 8
    - (G) ⁻2
    - (H) ⁻11
    - (J) ⁻17

STOP

Name _____   Date _____

● Lesson 2: Number Concepts

Directions: Read and work each problem. Find the correct answer. Fill in the circle that corresponds to your choice.

Examples

A. Four hundred thirty-thousand =

   (A) 40,300

   (B) 4,030

   (C) 430,000

   (D) 4,300,000

B. What is 0.068 rounded to the nearest tenth?

   (F) 0.1

   (G) 0.7

   (H) 0.6

   (J) 0.06

Clue Be sure the answer space you fill in is the same letter as the answer you think is correct. Key words, numbers, pictures, and figures will help you find the answers.

● Practice

1. Which of these is a prime number?

   (A) 25

   (B) 29

   (C) 33

   (D) 51

2. How much would the value of 63,518 be decreased by replacing the 3 with a 4?

   (F) 100

   (G) 10

   (H) 1,000

   (J) 10,000

3. What number goes in for *x* to make the equation true?

$$2\frac{4}{7} - 1\frac{x}{7} = \frac{5}{7}$$

   (A) 7

   (B) 8

   (C) 6

   (D) 4

4. Which is the best estimate of 62.4 x 58.9?

   (F) 60 x 60

   (G) 65 x 55

   (H) 60 x 50

   (J) 65 x 60

5. Look at the number pattern below. Which number would be next in the pattern?

42, 51.8, 42.9, 52.7, 43.8, ____

   (A) 49.2

   (B) 53.6

   (C) 54.1

   (D) 54.6

GO ON

MATH: CONCEPTS

● Lesson 2: Number Concepts (cont.)

6. Make two 5-digit numbers using the digits 2, 5, 6, 9, and 7 exactly once in each number. What are the largest and the smallest numbers you can write?

   (F) 97,625 and 25,976
   (G) 97,265 and 25,967
   (H) 97,652 and 25,679
   (J) 94,573 and 24,479

7. What is 9,783,432 rounded to the nearest ten thousand?

   (A) 9,770,000
   (B) 9,780,000
   (C) 9,790,000
   (D) 9,790

8. Which of these is equivalent to $7 - (8 - 3)$?

   (F) $56 - 21$
   (G) $^-1 - 3$
   (H) $7 - 5$
   (J) $56 + 21$

9. What is the next number in the set of numbers 1, 2, 3, 5, 8, 13?

   (A) 7
   (B) 5
   (C) 8
   (D) 21

10. Compare the following products.

    39 x 62 and 93 x 26

    (F) same
    (G) different
    (H) answer unknown
    (J) not enough information given

11. What is the next number in the sequence of numbers?

    159.76, 163.72, 156.79, 160.75, 153.82

    (A) 157.12
    (B) 156.32
    (C) 157.78
    (D) 156.13

12. Seventy-two members of an astronomy club went on a field trip to Hadler Planetarium. All but three of them paid the $4.00 fee to use the large telescope. Which number sentence shows the total amount paid by all students to use the telescope?

    (F) $72 - (3 \times 4)$
    (G) $72 (4 - 3)$
    (H) $72 \times 4 - 3$
    (J) $(72 - 3) \times 4$

13. Which of these is not equal to the others?

    (A) 46%
    (B) $\frac{46}{100}$
    (C) 0.46
    (D) 4.6

GO ON

MATH: CONCEPTS

● Lesson 2: Number Concepts (cont.)

14. Which of the following equations is not equivalent to the other three?

    (F) $x = 28 - 7$

    (G) $7 + x = 28$

    (H) $x - 28 = 7$

    (J) $x + 7 = 28$

15. There are five officers in the 8th grade class. Two are boys and three are girls. If a committee is chosen to include one boy and one girl to represent the school on the all-district council, how many different committees are possible?

    (A) 3

    (B) 5

    (C) 6

    (D) 8

16. If you have 2 pairs of jeans and 5 different T-shirts, how many different outfits do you have by picking a pair of jeans and a T-shirt?

    (F) 7

    (G) 10

    (H) 3

    (J) 12

17. Which of these statements is correct?

    (A) $c + ab = (a + b) - c$

    (B) $ab + cb = b (a + c)$

    (C) $ac + bc = (a + c) b$

    (D) $a - c = b - a$

18. What is the next number in this sequence?

    56.07, 57.02, 57.87, 58.62, 59.27

    (F) 59.82

    (G) 59.92

    (H) 57.02

    (J) 59.97

19. How much would the value of 472,868 increase if the 7 were changed to a 9?

    (A) 20,000

    (B) 2,000

    (C) 200,000

    (D) 200

20. Which is equal in value to 27%?

    (F) 2.7

    (G) 0.027

    (H) 0.270%

    (J) 0.27

21. What is 10,287,648 rounded to the nearest ten thousand?

    (A) 10,280,000

    (B) 10,300,000

    (C) 10,290,000

    (D) 10,285,000

STOP

Name _____ Date_____

MATH: CONCEPTS

● Lesson 3: Fractions and Decimals

Directions: Read and work each problem. Find the correct answer. Fill in the circle that corresponds to your choice.

Examples

A. 2.10 =

    (A) $\frac{10}{100}$

    (B) $\frac{21}{100}$

    (C) 21

    (D) $\frac{210}{100}$

B. Which of these is greater than the others?

    (F) two and one fourth

    (G) four fifths

    (H) two and one eighth

    (J) two and four hundredths

Clue Pay close attention to the numbers in the problem and in the answer choices. If you misread even one number, you will probably choose the wrong answer. If a problem is too difficult, skip it and come back to it later, if you have time.

● Practice

1. Which decimal gives the best estimate of the amount of the circle below that is shaded?

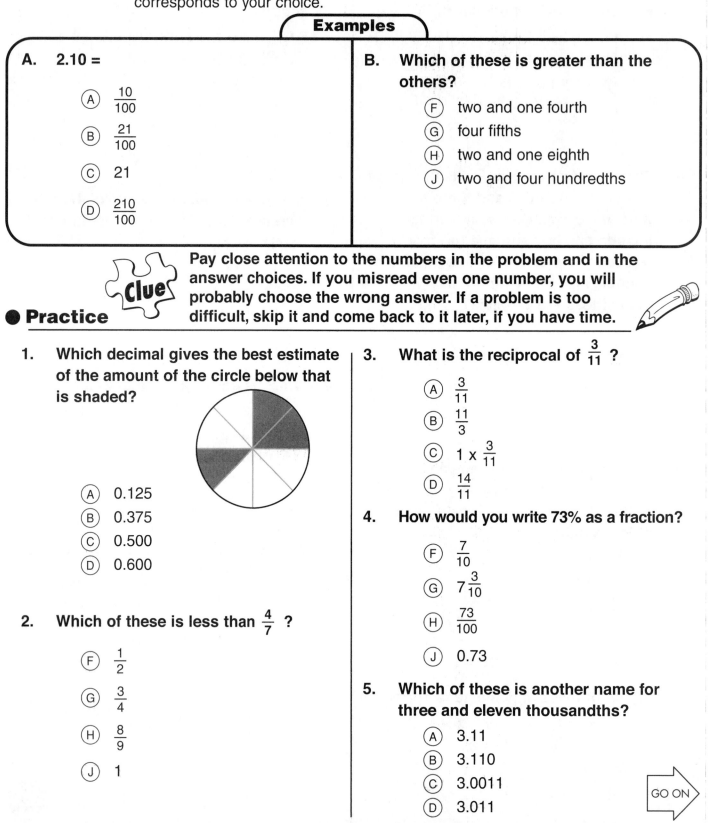

    (A) 0.125

    (B) 0.375

    (C) 0.500

    (D) 0.600

2. Which of these is less than $\frac{4}{7}$?

    (F) $\frac{1}{2}$

    (G) $\frac{3}{4}$

    (H) $\frac{8}{9}$

    (J) 1

3. What is the reciprocal of $\frac{3}{11}$?

    (A) $\frac{3}{11}$

    (B) $\frac{11}{3}$

    (C) $1 \times \frac{3}{11}$

    (D) $\frac{14}{11}$

4. How would you write 73% as a fraction?

    (F) $\frac{7}{10}$

    (G) $7\frac{3}{10}$

    (H) $\frac{73}{100}$

    (J) 0.73

5. Which of these is another name for three and eleven thousandths?

    (A) 3.11

    (B) 3.110

    (C) 3.0011

    (D) 3.011

GO ON

1-57768-978-X *Spectrum Test Practice 8*

━━━━━ MATH: CONCEPTS ━━━━━

● **Lesson 3: Fractions and Decimals (cont.)**

6. Which of these is the simplest name for $\frac{18}{90}$?

  (F) $\frac{9}{10}$

  (G) $\frac{3}{14}$

  (H) $\frac{1}{10}$

  (J) $\frac{1}{5}$

7. What is another name for $3\frac{5}{11}$?

  (A) $\frac{38}{5}$

  (B) $\frac{33}{5}$

  (C) $\frac{38}{11}$

  (D) $\frac{33}{11}$

8. What is the least common denominator for $\frac{2}{3}$, $\frac{7}{12}$, and $\frac{29}{36}$?

  (F) 27

  (G) 72

  (H) 24

  (J) 36

9. What is 0.038 expressed as a percent?

  (A) 38%

  (B) 3.8%

  (C) 0.38%

  (D) 0.038%

10. In this number line, P points closest to

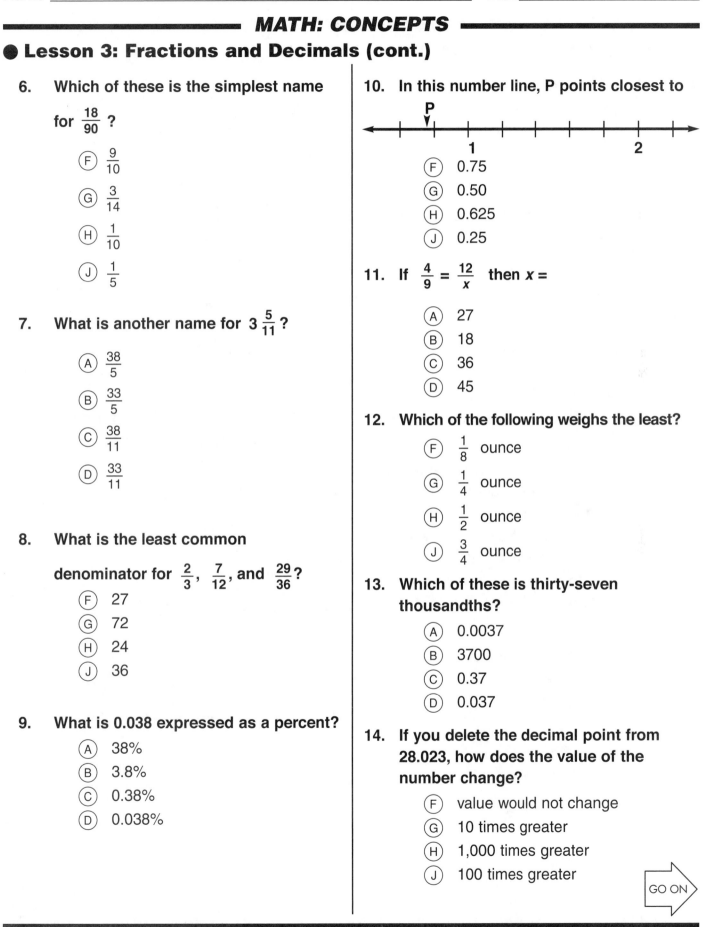

  (F) 0.75

  (G) 0.50

  (H) 0.625

  (J) 0.25

11. If $\frac{4}{9} = \frac{12}{x}$ then $x =$

  (A) 27

  (B) 18

  (C) 36

  (D) 45

12. Which of the following weighs the least?

  (F) $\frac{1}{8}$ ounce

  (G) $\frac{1}{4}$ ounce

  (H) $\frac{1}{2}$ ounce

  (J) $\frac{3}{4}$ ounce

13. Which of these is thirty-seven thousandths?

  (A) 0.0037

  (B) 3700

  (C) 0.37

  (D) 0.037

14. If you delete the decimal point from 28.023, how does the value of the number change?

  (F) value would not change

  (G) 10 times greater

  (H) 1,000 times greater

  (J) 100 times greater

GO ON

MATH: CONCEPTS

● Lesson 3: Fractions and Decimals (cont.)

15. How would you write 0.7% as a decimal?
- (A) 7.00
- (B) 0.07
- (C) 0.007
- (D) 0.7

16. Which of these decimal equivalents is incorrect?
- (F) $\frac{1}{4} = 0.25$
- (G) $\frac{3}{8} = 0.375$
- (H) $\frac{1}{8} = 0.367$
- (J) $\frac{5}{8} = 0.625$

17. Which of these statements is true?
- (A) A fraction is a division problem.
- (B) The number with the largest value should always appear on the far right.
- (C) It makes no difference where the decimal place is located.
- (D) Moving the decimal point one place to the left increases the value of the number.

18. Which of these decimals has the greatest value?
- (F) 17.6171
- (G) 17.6239
- (H) 17.6327
- (J) 17.638

19. Which of these decimals has the least value?
- (A) 0.082
- (B) 0.0082
- (C) 0.8
- (D) 0.802

20. Which of these statements is incorrect?
- (F) The denominator of a fraction tells how many equal parts to divide the whole into.
- (G) The numerator tells how many of the equal parts are to be counted.
- (H) A mixed fraction means a number of wholes and a part of one whole.
- (J) Improper fractions do not make much sense.

21. Which of these fractions is not equal to $\frac{2}{3}$?
- (A) $\frac{18}{27}$
- (B) $\frac{32}{48}$
- (C) $\frac{8}{12}$
- (D) $\frac{64}{72}$

22. Which of these represents the least value?
- (F) $\frac{4}{9}$
- (G) 22%
- (H) 0.18
- (J) 0.436

STOP

Name _____ Date_____

MATH: CONCEPTS
SAMPLE TEST

● **Directions:** Read each problem. Mark the answer you think is correct.

Examples

A. If you estimate by rounding to whole

numbers, what is $6.21 + 9\frac{3}{4}$?

- (A) 6 + 10
- (B) 7 + 9
- (C) 7 + 10
- (D) 6 + 9

B. What is the greatest common factor of 24 and 36?

- (F) 6
- (G) 12
- (H) 18
- (J) 3

---

1. The absolute value of ⁻37 is

- (A) $\sqrt{37}$
- (B) $\frac{1}{37}$
- (C) 37
- (D) 37^2

2. 8 x 9 – 8 =

- (F) ⁻72
- (G) 8
- (H) 64
- (J) 80

3. Which of these fractions is closest to 1?

- (A) $\frac{3}{5}$
- (B) $\frac{1}{2}$
- (C) $\frac{2}{3}$
- (D) $\frac{2}{9}$

4. What number completes this number sentence 3 x _____ = 90 x 30?

- (F) 9
- (G) 90
- (H) 300
- (J) 900

5. $9^3 – 84 =$

- (A) 84
- (B) ⁻729
- (C) 81
- (D) 645

6. Which point is closest to $3\frac{3}{4}$ on this number line?

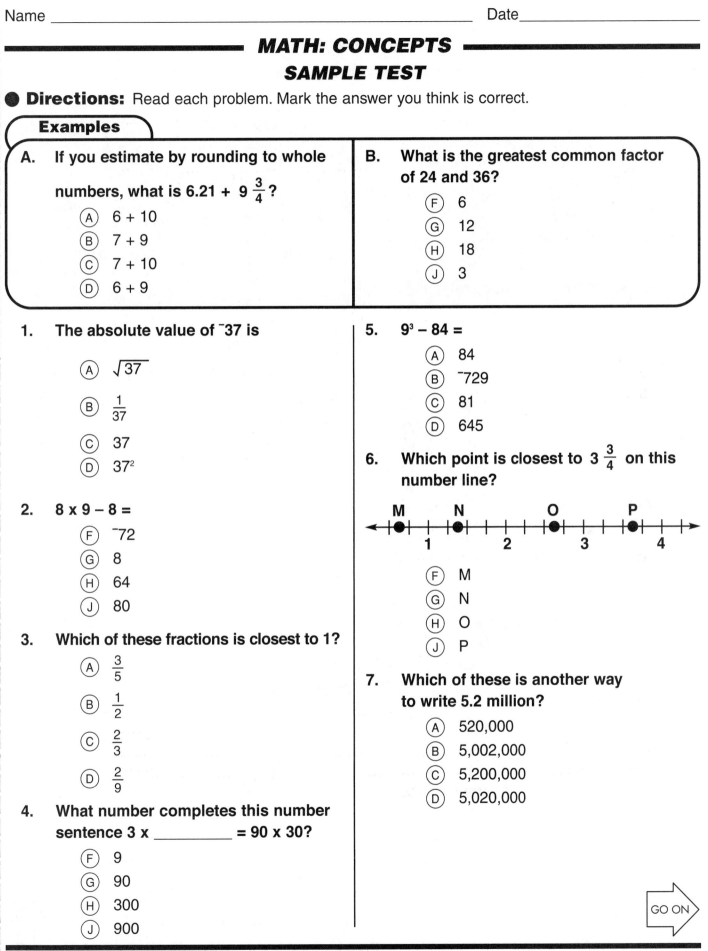

- (F) M
- (G) N
- (H) O
- (J) P

7. Which of these is another way to write 5.2 million?

- (A) 520,000
- (B) 5,002,000
- (C) 5,200,000
- (D) 5,020,000

GO ON

MATH: CONCEPTS
SAMPLE TEST (cont.)

8. Which of these is another way to write 700 + 10 + 0.06?

    (F) 70,010.06

    (G)   701.06

    (H)   710.06

    (J)   700.106

9. Which of these is not equal in value to the others?

    (A) 7%

    (B) 0.07

    (C) 0.007

    (D) $\frac{7}{100}$

10. Which of these percentages gives the best estimate for the amount of the circle that is not shaded?

    (F) 50%

    (G) 30%

    (H) 70%

    (J) 90%

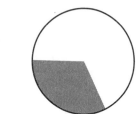

11. The drama club set a goal of $1,000 for its Spring Drama Drive. However, they collected $2,460 altogether. What percent of its goal did the drama club collect?

    (A) 100%

    (B) 246%

    (C) 24.6%

    (D) 2.46%

12. In the numeral 3,860,100, what is the value of the 6?

    (F) 6 hundred

    (G) 6 thousand

    (H) 60 thousand

    (J) 6 hundred thousand

13. Which of these is between 0.0036 and 0.05?

    (A) 0.150

    (B) 0.015

    (C) 0.0018

    (D) 0.501

14. What is another way to write 6^4?

    (F) 6 x 6 x 6

    (G) 6 x 6 x 6 x 6

    (H) 6 x 6 x 6 x 6 x 6

    (J) $\sqrt{6}$

15.
    $^-15$
    $+\ 4$

    (A) $^-19$

    (B) $^-11$

    (C) 11

    (D) 19

16. Which of these numbers is a prime number?

    (F) 47

    (G) 49

    (H) 54

    (J) 72

GO ON

17. Which of these decimals has the greatest value?

    (A) 7.13

    (B) 7.24

    (C) 7.90

    (D) 7.032

18. Which fraction has the least value?

    (F) $\frac{3}{5}$

    (G) $\frac{8}{25}$

    (H) $\frac{5}{9}$

    (J) $\frac{7}{8}$

19. Which group of integers goes from greatest to least?

    (A) $^-6, ^-4, 2, 0, 8$

    (B) $^-3, ^-5, 0, ^-4, 2$

    (C) $6, 2, 0, ^-1, 4$

    (D) $7, 3, 1, ^-4, ^-8$

20. What is the value of the expression: $25 \div (16 - 11)$?

    (F) 25

    (G) 5

    (H) 15

    (J) 50

21. Forty-seven boys and fifty-one girls were in the 8th grade class. Which estimate comes closest to the fraction that represents boys in the class?

    (A) $\frac{3}{4}$

    (B) $\frac{1}{2}$

    (C) $\frac{5}{8}$

    (D) $\frac{7}{8}$

22. Which of these statements is true?

    (F) $a(b + c) = ab + ac$

    (G) $ac + b = a(b + c)$

    (H) $a(b - c) = bc - a$

    (J) $ab - bc = a(b + c)$

23. Which of these statements is true?

    (A) $a + b - c = c - a + b$

    (B) $a \div b = b \div a$

    (C) $b + c + a = c + a + b$

    (D) $ba \div c = bc \div a$

24. Which of these statements is not true?

    (F) $a(b + c) = ab + ac$

    (G) $a + b + c = c + a + b$

    (H) $(a \times b) \times c = a \times (b \times c)$

    (J) $(a - b) - c = a - (b - c)$

STOP

MATH: COMPUTATION

● Lesson 4: Whole Numbers

Directions: Mark the space for the correct answer to each.

Examples

A.
```
   300
   846
 + 197
```
Ⓐ 1,433
Ⓑ 1,343
Ⓒ 1,822
Ⓓ 1,386

B.
```
   847
 −  54
```
Ⓕ 690
Ⓖ 793
Ⓗ 789
Ⓗ 436

Clue If the answer you find is not one of the answer choices, rework the problem on scratch paper.

● Practice

1.
```
  6,154
 − 1,826
```
Ⓐ 4,614
Ⓑ 4,418
Ⓒ 4,328
Ⓓ 4,238

5.
```
   658
 −  91
```
Ⓐ 749
Ⓑ 567
Ⓒ 647
Ⓓ 869

2.
```
    68
  x 29
```
Ⓕ 1,972
Ⓖ 1,942
Ⓗ 1,868
Ⓙ 1,912

6.
```
  20,002
  x  501
```
Ⓕ 10,021,002
Ⓖ 2,042,002
Ⓗ 14,342,00
Ⓙ 12,002,002

3. 148⟌5,328
Ⓐ 36 R 8
Ⓑ 36 R 3
Ⓒ 35 R 2
Ⓓ 36

7. 54⟌756
Ⓐ 16
Ⓑ 24
Ⓒ 12
Ⓓ 14

4.
```
   866
 +  61
```
Ⓕ 627
Ⓖ 927
Ⓗ 917
Ⓙ 1017

8.
```
   234
   345
 + 868
```
Ⓕ 1,268
Ⓖ 1,447
Ⓗ 1,362
Ⓙ 2,447

GO ON

Name _____   Date_____

MATH: COMPUTATION

● **Lesson 4: Whole Numbers (cont.)**

9. 62)‾23,415
   - Ⓐ 377 R 41
   - Ⓑ 467 R 3
   - Ⓒ 473 R 12
   - Ⓓ 503 R 17

13. 87,211
    − 23,334
   - Ⓐ 73,807
   - Ⓑ 67,007
   - Ⓒ 63,877
   - Ⓓ 43,117

10. 66,577
    x 88
   - Ⓕ 1,418,012
   - Ⓖ 4,136,416
   - Ⓗ 5,476,166
   - Ⓙ 5,858,776

14. 834,521
    + 766,942
   - Ⓕ 1,601,363
   - Ⓖ 1,601,463
   - Ⓗ 2,006,343
   - Ⓙ 3,116,041

15. 679)‾6,004,598
   - Ⓐ 7,635 R101
   - Ⓑ 8,843 R20
   - Ⓒ 8,348 R12
   - Ⓓ 7,536 R110

11. 513,420
    − 389,011
   - Ⓐ 214,109
   - Ⓑ 124,409
   - Ⓒ 125,509
   - Ⓓ 105,409

16. 26,404
    x 42
   - Ⓕ 1,108,968
   - Ⓖ 1,218,412
   - Ⓗ 1,208,968
   - Ⓙ 1,112,408

12. 152,897
    + 98,004
   - Ⓕ 250,901
   - Ⓖ 240,901
   - Ⓗ 250,091
   - Ⓙ 240,991

17. 3,462,018
    − 976,554
   - Ⓐ 1,242,814
   - Ⓑ 2,518,033
   - Ⓒ 2,485,464
   - Ⓓ 2,143,244

STOP

MATH: COMPUTATION

● Lesson 5: Decimals

Directions: Mark the space for the correct answer to each problem.

Examples

A. 24.342
   – 3.797

  Ⓐ 22.032
  Ⓑ 19.846
  Ⓒ 20.545
  Ⓓ 19.322

B. 0.82
   + 0.273

  Ⓕ 0.994
  Ⓖ 1.122
  Ⓗ 1.211
  Ⓙ 1.093

Clue Pay close attention when you are dividing or multiplying decimals. It is easy to make a mistake by misplacing the decimal point.

● Practice

1. $2.8\overline{)2.1588}$
  Ⓐ 1.042
  Ⓑ 0.771
  Ⓒ 1.141
  Ⓓ 2.043

5. 341.050
  – 10.623
  Ⓐ 143.227
  Ⓑ 232.127
  Ⓒ 330.427
  Ⓓ 132.127

2. 22.22
  – 9.999
  Ⓕ 12.221
  Ⓖ 1.212
  Ⓗ 1.341
  Ⓙ 4214

6. $.305\overline{).024766}$
  Ⓕ 0.0812
  Ⓖ 0.1412
  Ⓗ 0.812
  Ⓙ 1.0184

3. .039
  x .009
  Ⓐ 0.351
  Ⓑ 351
  Ⓒ 0.00351
  Ⓓ 0.000351

7. .3551
  x .208
  Ⓐ 0.0492816
  Ⓑ 0.0738608
  Ⓒ 0.0941512
  Ⓓ 0.0512733

4. 40.092
  + 63.98
  Ⓕ 104.072
  Ⓖ 200.12
  Ⓗ 142.212
  Ⓙ 186.122

8. 2.04
  3.86
  8.45
  + 9.99
  Ⓕ 18.34
  Ⓖ 24.18
  Ⓗ 24.34
  Ⓙ 34.43

GO ON

MATH: COMPUTATION

● Lesson 5: Decimals (cont.)

9.
```
   38.042
   93.586
 + 63.108
```
- Ⓐ 1947.36
- Ⓑ 19.4736
- Ⓒ 194.736
- Ⓓ 0.194736

14.
```
  40.092
+ 63.98
```
- Ⓕ 104.072
- Ⓖ 106.068
- Ⓗ 104.720
- Ⓙ 927.550

10.
```
   3.08
 x 3.08
```
- Ⓕ 11.4328
- Ⓖ 9.4864
- Ⓗ 10.4828
- Ⓙ 9.3636

15.
```
  .438
x .177
```
- Ⓐ 0.077526
- Ⓑ 0.070256
- Ⓒ 0.000726
- Ⓓ 0.072056

11.
```
   2.005
 - .9999
```
- Ⓐ 1.0060
- Ⓑ 1.0001
- Ⓒ 1.0360
- Ⓓ 1.0051

16.
```
  341.050
-  10.623
```
- Ⓕ 330.427
- Ⓖ 313.217
- Ⓗ 303.401
- Ⓙ 331.421

12. .81)‾43.254‾
- Ⓕ 534.2
- Ⓖ 53.4
- Ⓗ 0.5342
- Ⓙ 5.342

17.
```
  67.123
+ 62.467
```
- Ⓐ 129.59
- Ⓑ 1.04072
- Ⓒ 10.4007
- Ⓓ 111.122

13. 41.8)‾1185.866‾
- Ⓐ 28.37
- Ⓑ 38.72
- Ⓒ 42.19
- Ⓓ 27.46

STOP

1-57768-978-X Spectrum Test Practice 8

MATH: COMPUTATION

● Lesson 6: Percent

Directions: Mark the space for the correct answer to each problem.

Examples

A. What is 20% of 35?

- (A) 700
- (B) 7
- (C) 17
- (D) 4

B. How much is 46% of 4?

- (F) 1.42
- (G) 1.84
- (H) 2.20
- (J) 2.28

Clue Pay close attention to where you place the decimal point in percent problems. It is easy to place it in the wrong place.

● Practice

1. What is 80% of 40?

- (A) 32
- (B) 320
- (C) .32
- (D) 3.20

2. What percent of 96 is 17.28?

- (F) 1.8%
- (G) 18%
- (H) 28%
- (J) 2.8%

3. 66 is what percent of 30?

- (A) 11%
- (B) 20%
- (C) 120%
- (D) 220%

4. What percent of 40 is 14?

- (F) 35%
- (G) 25%
- (H) 15%
- (J) 45%

5. How much is 72% of 6?

- (A) 5.04
- (B) 2.14
- (C) 4.32
- (D) 5.85

6. 38% of 45 is how much?

- (F) 42.3
- (G) 28.6
- (H) 17.1
- (J) 14.3

7. How much is 5% of 17?

- (A) .94
- (B) .85
- (C) 1.4
- (D) 7.2

8. How much is 1.5% of 900?

- (F) 33.2
- (G) 13.5
- (H) 88.9
- (J) 12.0

GO ON

Name _____   Date_____

MATH: COMPUTATION

● Lesson 6: Percent (cont.)

9. 130% of 7 is how much?

(A) 7
(B) 17.2
(C) 9.1
(D) 8.0

10. $\frac{3}{4}$ is expressed as

(F) 40%
(G) 75%
(H) 25%
(J) 60%

11. .35 is expressed as

(A) 35%
(B) 3.5%
(C) 0.35%
(D) 350%

12. Which percent is largest?

(F) 2.8%
(G) 28%
(H) 280%
(J) 0.28%

13. How much is 250% of 20?

(A) 20
(B) 40
(C) 50
(D) 60

14. How much is 70% of 15?

(F) 7.5
(G) 8.2
(H) 10.5
(J) 12.0

15. What percent of 90 is 8.1?

(A) 9%
(B) 11%
(C) 13%
(D) 8%

16. 15 out of 48 is about—

(F) 0.3%
(G) 3%
(H) 30%
(J) 300%

17. 7 is 140% of about—

(A) 50
(B) 5
(C) 20
(D) 2

STOP

1-57768-978-X *Spectrum Test Practice 8*

Name _____   Date_____

MATH COMPUTATION

● Lesson 7: Fractions and Mixed Numbers

Directions: Mark the space for the correct answer to each problem.

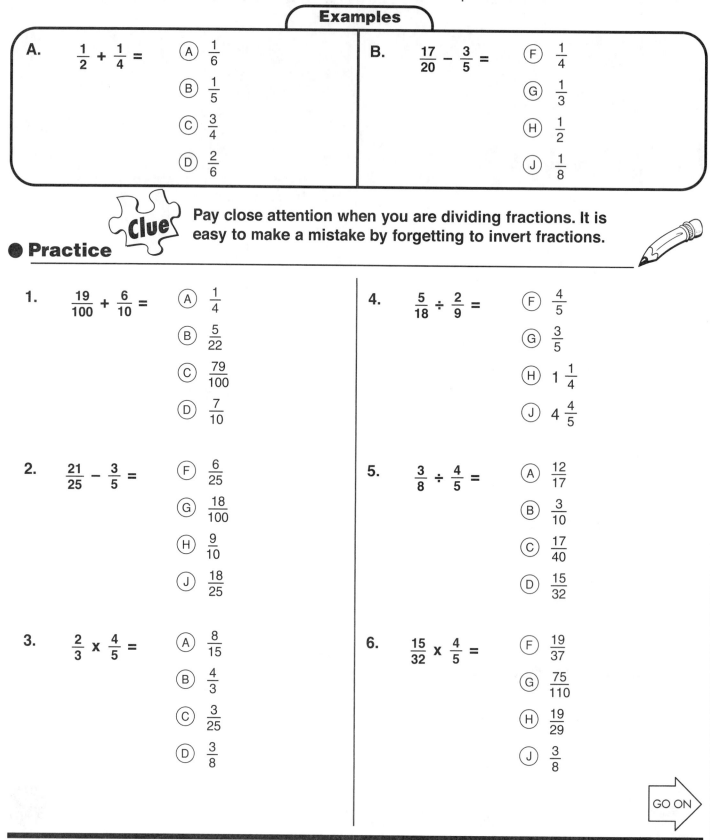

Examples

A. $\frac{1}{2} + \frac{1}{4} =$

(A) $\frac{1}{6}$

(B) $\frac{1}{5}$

(C) $\frac{3}{4}$

(D) $\frac{2}{6}$

B. $\frac{17}{20} - \frac{3}{5} =$

(F) $\frac{1}{4}$

(G) $\frac{1}{3}$

(H) $\frac{1}{2}$

(J) $\frac{1}{8}$

Clue Pay close attention when you are dividing fractions. It is easy to make a mistake by forgetting to invert fractions.

● Practice

1. $\frac{19}{100} + \frac{6}{10} =$

(A) $\frac{1}{4}$

(B) $\frac{5}{22}$

(C) $\frac{79}{100}$

(D) $\frac{7}{10}$

2. $\frac{21}{25} - \frac{3}{5} =$

(F) $\frac{6}{25}$

(G) $\frac{18}{100}$

(H) $\frac{9}{10}$

(J) $\frac{18}{25}$

3. $\frac{2}{3} \times \frac{4}{5} =$

(A) $\frac{8}{15}$

(B) $\frac{4}{3}$

(C) $\frac{3}{25}$

(D) $\frac{3}{8}$

4. $\frac{5}{18} \div \frac{2}{9} =$

(F) $\frac{4}{5}$

(G) $\frac{3}{5}$

(H) $1\frac{1}{4}$

(J) $4\frac{4}{5}$

5. $\frac{3}{8} \div \frac{4}{5} =$

(A) $\frac{12}{17}$

(B) $\frac{3}{10}$

(C) $\frac{17}{40}$

(D) $\frac{15}{32}$

6. $\frac{15}{32} \times \frac{4}{5} =$

(F) $\frac{19}{37}$

(G) $\frac{75}{110}$

(H) $\frac{19}{29}$

(J) $\frac{3}{8}$

GO ON

108   1-57768-978-X *Spectrum Test Practice 8*

MATH COMPUTATION

● Fractions and Mixed Numbers (cont.)

7. $\frac{5}{6} + \frac{5}{8} =$

Ⓐ $\frac{3}{7}$

Ⓑ $1\frac{11}{24}$

Ⓒ $1\frac{7}{8}$

Ⓓ $1\frac{3}{8}$

8. $\frac{7}{8} - \frac{3}{12} =$

Ⓕ $\frac{5}{24}$

Ⓖ $\frac{5}{8}$

Ⓗ $\frac{21}{60}$

Ⓙ $\frac{4}{15}$

9. $\frac{5}{9} \div \frac{4}{5} =$

Ⓐ $\frac{20}{14}$

Ⓑ $\frac{25}{36}$

Ⓒ $\frac{3}{4}$

Ⓓ $\frac{5}{8}$

10. $3\frac{1}{4} - 2\frac{3}{4} =$

Ⓕ $\frac{1}{3}$

Ⓖ $\frac{3}{8}$

Ⓗ $\frac{1}{2}$

Ⓙ $\frac{3}{4}$

11. $\frac{1}{2} + 1\frac{1}{8} =$

Ⓐ $1\frac{5}{8}$

Ⓑ $1\frac{3}{8}$

Ⓒ $2\frac{1}{2}$

Ⓓ $2\frac{1}{4}$

12. $\frac{13}{48} \times 2 =$

Ⓕ $\frac{4}{9}$

Ⓖ $\frac{3}{8}$

Ⓗ $\frac{13}{24}$

Ⓙ $\frac{5}{13}$

13. $\frac{7}{8} \div \frac{7}{8} =$

Ⓐ $\frac{7}{8}$

Ⓑ $\frac{8}{7}$

Ⓒ 1

Ⓓ $1\frac{1}{8}$

14. $\frac{23}{8} \times \frac{1}{3} =$

Ⓕ $\frac{23}{24}$

Ⓖ $\frac{17}{24}$

Ⓗ $\frac{11}{12}$

Ⓙ $\frac{3}{11}$

15. $1\frac{1}{8} + \frac{3}{4} =$

Ⓐ $1\frac{1}{3}$

Ⓑ $1\frac{1}{2}$

Ⓒ $1\frac{3}{4}$

Ⓓ $1\frac{7}{8}$

16. $3\frac{1}{2} - 3\frac{1}{4} =$

Ⓕ $\frac{1}{8}$

Ⓖ $\frac{1}{4}$

Ⓗ $\frac{3}{4}$

Ⓙ $\frac{3}{8}$

STOP

Name _____ Date _____

MATH: COMPUTATION
SAMPLE TEST

● **Directions:** Mark the space for the correct answer to each problem.

Examples

A. $20 \overline{\smash{)}\,500}$

- (A) 2500
- (B) 250
- (C) 42
- (D) none of these

B. $0.6 \div 0.25 =$

- (F) 2.4
- (G) 24
- (H) 0.2
- (J) none of these

---

1. $3.372 \div 0.6 =$
- (A) 5.620
- (B) 0.562
- (C) 0.056
- (D) 0.006

5. $392 \times 67 =$
- (A) 2626.4
- (B) 26,264
- (C) 26,164
- (D) 5.85

2. $36 + {}^-45 =$
- (F) 9
- (G) $^-9$
- (H) 81
- (J) $^-81$

6. $25^3 =$
- (F) 625
- (G) 15,625
- (H) 15,675
- (J) none of the above

3. $7(5 - 8) =$
- (A) 21
- (B) $^-21$
- (C) 27
- (D) $^-91$

7. $1.72 \times .34 =$
- (A) 584.4
- (B) 58.48
- (C) 5.848
- (D) 0.5848

8. $\frac{3}{8} \div \frac{4}{5} =$
- (F) $\frac{15}{32}$
- (G) $\frac{3}{10}$
- (H) $\frac{17}{40}$
- (J) $1\frac{5}{8}$

4. $3\frac{5}{6} + 5\frac{1}{4} =$
- (F) $8\frac{5}{6}$
- (G) 9
- (H) $9\frac{1}{12}$
- (J) $9\frac{1}{6}$

GO ON ▷

1-57768-978-X Spectrum Test Practice 8

MATH: COMPUTATION
SAMPLE TEST (cont.)

9. 10% of $47.00 =
    - (A) $4.70
    - (B) $0.37
    - (C) $0.47
    - (D) none of these

10. 3807.60 − 0.23 =
    - (F) 3807.33
    - (G) 3807.4
    - (H) 3807.43
    - (J) none of these

11. 85% of __ = 68
    - (A) 8.0
    - (B) 0.80
    - (C) 60.0
    - (D) none of these

12. $2\frac{1}{3} + 4\frac{1}{6} + 5\frac{1}{4}$ =
    - (F) 12
    - (G) $11\frac{1}{2}$
    - (H) $11\frac{3}{4}$
    - (J) none of these

13. 82 ÷ 4 =
    - (A) 4
    - (B) 64
    - (C) 16
    - (D) none of these

14. ⁻30 x ⁻9 =
    - (F) ⁻270
    - (G) 270
    - (H) ⁻39
    - (J) none of these

15. $\frac{3}{4}$ x $\frac{1}{2}$ x $\frac{3}{5}$ =
    - (A) $\frac{7}{11}$
    - (B) $1\frac{17}{20}$
    - (C) $\frac{9}{40}$
    - (D) none of these

16. $5\frac{1}{2}$ x $3\frac{1}{6}$ =
    - (F) $8\frac{2}{3}$
    - (G) $17\frac{5}{12}$
    - (H) $15\frac{1}{12}$
    - (J) $15\frac{2}{3}$

GO ON

17.   9.72
    + 15.969

(A) 25.689
(B) 2.568
(C) 25.698
(D) 2.5698

22. 14$\overline{)28,028}$

(F) 2,002
(G) 20,020
(H) 2,020
(J) 20,200

18. 42$\overline{)12.222}$

(F) 2.910
(G) 0.291
(H) 0.289
(J) 2.890

23. **What percent of the bar is darkened?**

(A) 30%
(B) 50%
(C) 70%
(D) 90%

19. $\frac{11}{12} - \frac{1}{4} =$

(A) $\frac{10}{12}$
(B) $\frac{8}{12}$
(C) $\frac{3}{4}$
(D) $1\frac{1}{4}$

24. **What percent of the bar is darkened?**

(F) 5%
(G) 20%
(H) 40%
(J) 80%

20. $\frac{3}{5} \times \frac{1}{10} \times \frac{1}{2} =$

(F) $\frac{3}{100}$
(G) $\frac{3}{10}$
(H) $\frac{5}{100}$
(J) $\frac{25}{10}$

21.   78,212
       4,987
    + 12,735

(A) 92,484
(B) 93,933
(C) 95,234
(D) 95,934

STOP

Name _____   Date _____

MATH: APPLICATIONS

● **Lesson 8: Geometry**

Directions: Find the correct answer to each geometry problem. Fill in the circle that corresponds to your choice.

┌─ **Example** ─┐

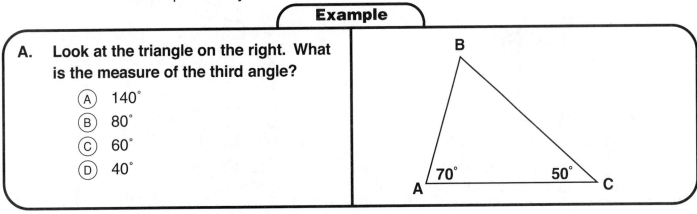

A. **Look at the triangle on the right. What is the measure of the third angle?**

  Ⓐ 140°
  Ⓑ 80°
  Ⓒ 60°
  Ⓓ 40°

Clue — Read the question carefully and think about what you are supposed to do. Look for key words, numbers, and figures before you choose an answer.

● **Practice**

1. **The map below shows the distances between six cities in Pima County. Suppose you wanted to go from Mathtown to Circleville. What is the shortest distance you must travel?**

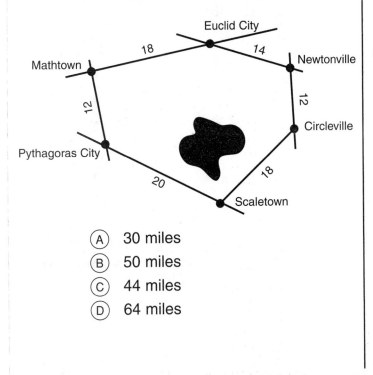

  Ⓐ 30 miles
  Ⓑ 50 miles
  Ⓒ 44 miles
  Ⓓ 64 miles

2. **What is the volume of a freezer that is 5 feet high, 4 feet wide, and 3 feet deep?**

  Ⓕ 42 ft.³
  Ⓖ 58 ft.³
  Ⓗ 60 ft.³
  Ⓙ 72 ft.³

3. **Which number sentence shows how to find the area of a lawn that is 10 yards by 20 yards?**

  Ⓐ area = 2 x 10 yd. + 2 x 20 yd.
  Ⓑ area = 10 yd. x 20 yd.
  Ⓒ area = 10 ft. x 20 ft.
  Ⓓ 86 square meters

4. **Which of these is an acute angle?**

  Ⓕ 90°
  Ⓖ 118°
  Ⓗ 15°
  Ⓙ 0°

GO ON ▷

MATH: APPLICATIONS

● Lesson 8: Geometry (cont.)

5. Which of the following best expresses the size of the solid below?

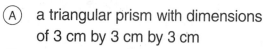

Ⓐ a triangular prism with dimensions of 3 cm by 3 cm by 3 cm

Ⓑ a cube with dimensions of 3 cm by 3 cm by 3 cm

Ⓒ a rectangular prism with dimensions of 3 cm by 6 cm by 3 cm

Ⓓ a cube with dimensions of 3 cm by 6 cm by 3 cm

6. What is the volume of the solid found in number 5?

Ⓕ 27 cm²

Ⓖ 27 cm³

Ⓗ 54 cm²

Ⓙ 54 cm³

7. Which of these statements is not true?

Ⓐ Two rays make up an angle.

Ⓑ Perpendicular lines intersect.

Ⓒ A right angle contains 90˚.

Ⓓ Parallel lines meet only at a 90˚ angle.

8. Find the area of the figure below:

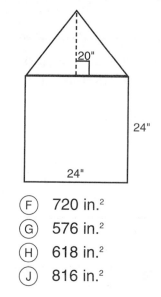

Ⓕ 720 in.²

Ⓖ 576 in.²

Ⓗ 618 in.²

Ⓙ 816 in.²

9. What is the area of this 16-inch pizza? (A 16-inch pizza has a 16-inch diameter.)

Ⓐ 50.24 in.²

Ⓑ 200.96 in.²

Ⓒ 100.48 in.²

Ⓓ 803.84 in.²

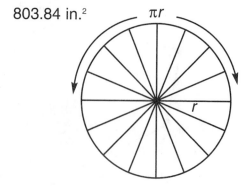

10. A 16-inch pizza costs $13.99. Find the cost per square inch to the nearest cent.

Ⓕ $0.02

Ⓖ $0.06

Ⓗ $0.07

Ⓙ $0.14

GO ON

● Lesson 8: Geometry (cont.)

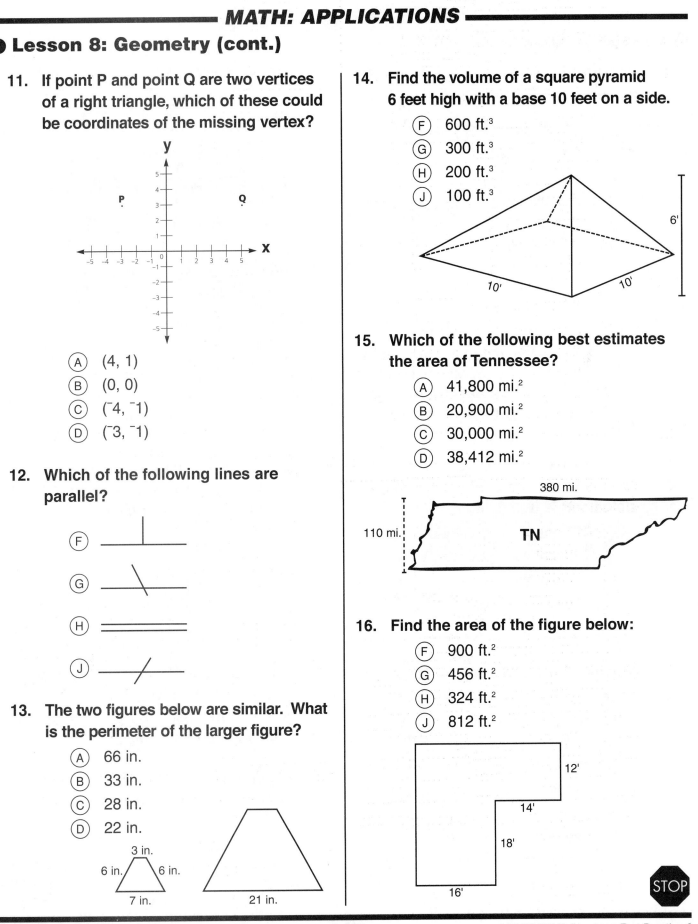

11. If point P and point Q are two vertices of a right triangle, which of these could be coordinates of the missing vertex?

    (A) (4, 1)
    (B) (0, 0)
    (C) (⁻4, ⁻1)
    (D) (⁻3, ⁻1)

12. Which of the following lines are parallel?

    (F)
    (G)
    (H)
    (J)

13. The two figures below are similar. What is the perimeter of the larger figure?

    (A) 66 in.
    (B) 33 in.
    (C) 28 in.
    (D) 22 in.

3 in.
6 in. / \ 6 in.
7 in.
21 in.

14. Find the volume of a square pyramid 6 feet high with a base 10 feet on a side.

    (F) 600 ft.³
    (G) 300 ft.³
    (H) 200 ft.³
    (J) 100 ft.³

6'
10'   10'

15. Which of the following best estimates the area of Tennessee?

    (A) 41,800 mi.²
    (B) 20,900 mi.²
    (C) 30,000 mi.²
    (D) 38,412 mi.²

380 mi.
110 mi.
TN

16. Find the area of the figure below:

    (F) 900 ft.²
    (G) 456 ft.²
    (H) 324 ft.²
    (J) 812 ft.²

12'
14'
18'
16'

STOP

MATH: APPLICATIONS

● **Lesson 9: Measurement**

Directions: Find the correct answer to each measurement problem. Fill in the circle that corresponds to your choice.

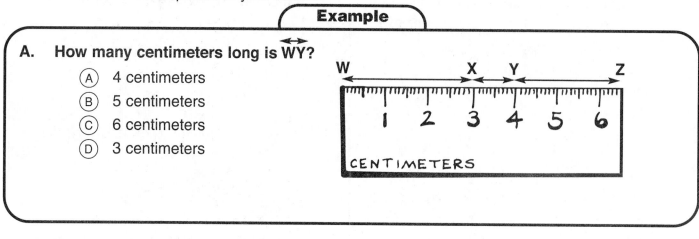

Example

A. How many centimeters long is $\overleftrightarrow{WY}$?

   Ⓐ 4 centimeters
   Ⓑ 5 centimeters
   Ⓒ 6 centimeters
   Ⓓ 3 centimeters

Clue

If you are confused by a problem, read it again. If you are still confused, skip the problem and come back to it later. For some problems, you will have to work on scratch paper. Be sure to transfer numbers accurately and compute carefully.

● **Practice**

1. Suppose you had 5 coins in your pocket totaling $0.53. Which of the following statements is true about the coins?

   Ⓐ Some of the coins are nickels.
   Ⓑ Two of the coins are dimes.
   Ⓒ Two of the coins are quarters.
   Ⓓ None of the coins are pennies.

2. Which of the following comes closest to the diameter of a dinner plate?

   Ⓕ 30 mm
   Ⓖ 30 cm
   Ⓗ 30 dm
   Ⓙ 30 m

3. Which of these is the greatest volume?

   Ⓐ 36 pints
   Ⓑ 24 quarts
   Ⓒ 4 gallons
   Ⓓ 60 cups

4. If you convert pounds to kilograms by dividing by 2.2, how many kg are there in a 10-pound bag of charcoal?

   Ⓕ 10 kg
   Ⓖ 8.6 kg
   Ⓗ 4.54 kg
   Ⓙ 3.63 kg

5. Which of the following comes closest to the estimate of the number of grams in two objects weighing 1,945 mg and 1,382 mg?

   Ⓐ 1 g
   Ⓑ 2 g
   Ⓒ 3 g
   Ⓓ 4 g

GO ON

MATH: APPLICATIONS

● Lesson 9: Measurement (cont.)

6. A bus was scheduled to leave the station at 3:15 P.M. Because of a rainstorm, the bus was delayed for 3 hours and 50 minutes. What time did the bus leave the station?

   F) 6:30 P.M.
   G) 6:50 P.M.
   H) 7:05 P.M.
   J) 7:15 P.M.

7. A worker had a roll of tape that was 10 yards long. She cut 7 feet of tape from the roll. How much tape was left on the roll?

   A) 8 yards
   B) 7 yards and 2 feet
   C) 6 yards and 2 feet
   D) 9 yards

8. How many inches are in 13 feet?

   F) 144
   G) 86
   H) 156
   J) 13

9. Which comes closest to the length of an unsharpened pencil?

   A) 6 inches
   B) 6 centimeters
   C) 6 millimeters
   D) 6 feet

10. Which of these would be purchased by the ton?

    F) gasoline
    G) gravel
    H) potatoes
    J) milk

11. Which of these rooms probably measures 12 feet by 11 feet?

    A) bathroom
    B) bedroom
    C) pantry
    D) hall closet

12. Which works best in measuring the height of a mountain?

    F) yards
    G) inches
    H) feet
    J) centimeters

13. What fraction of a yard is 27 inches?

    A) $\frac{1}{2}$
    B) $\frac{2}{3}$
    C) $\frac{3}{4}$
    D) $\frac{5}{6}$

14. Which comes closest to the length of a loaf of garlic bread?

    F) 1 meter
    G) 5 decimeters
    H) 180 millimeters
    J) 18 centimeters

15. 862 millimeters is equal to—

    A) 0.862 meters
    B) 8.620 meters
    C) 86.2 meters
    D) 0.0862 meters

STOP

Name _____   Date_____

MATH: APPLICATIONS

● Lesson 10: Problem Solving

Directions: Find the correct answer to each problem. Fill in the space that corresponds to your choice.

Examples

A. A lake is normally 42 feet deep. Which number sentence shows the depth after a storm makes the lake 3 feet deeper?

- (A) 42 − 3 = □
- (B) 42 + 3 = □
- (C) 42 x 3 = □
- (D) 42 ÷ 3 = □

B. Samuel bought 80 small baskets of tomatoes at $1.50 each and sold them for $4.00 each. How much did she make altogether?

- (F) $150
- (G) $200
- (H) $275
- (J) Not given

Clue Read each problem carefully. Look for key words, numbers, and figures on each problem. If you must work on scratch paper, be sure you perform the correct operation.

● Practice

1. Ten square tables, each seating one person per side, are pushed together to form one long rectangular table. How many people can be seated?

- (A) 20
- (B) 22
- (C) 24
- (D) 28

2. Terry has 6 blue shirts, 5 green shirts, and 3 striped shirts. If 2 of the blue shirts are also striped, how many shirts are there?

- (F) 14
- (G) 12
- (H) 10
- (J) 4

3. If the truck used 25 gallons of gas to travel 375 miles, how far can it go with 4 gallons?

- (A) 96 miles
- (B) 50 miles
- (C) 56 miles
- (D) 60 miles

4. Jason is 6 feet tall and casts a shadow of 5 feet. If he stands next to a tree that casts a 10-foot shadow, how tall is the tree?

- (F) 10 feet
- (G) 12 feet
- (H) 14 feet
- (J) 8 feet

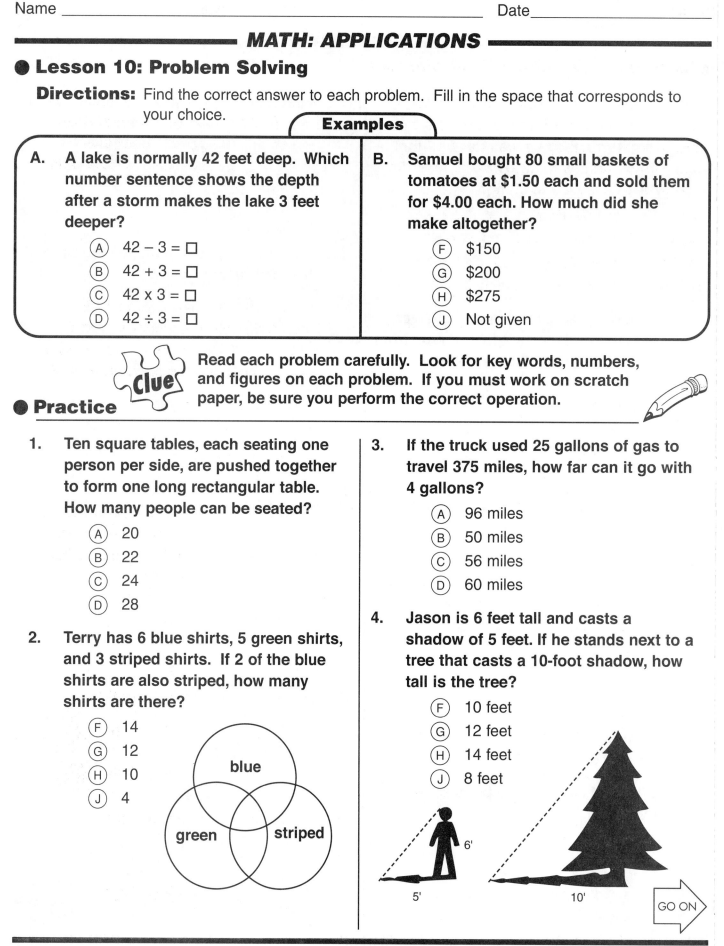

GO ON

MATH: APPLICATIONS

● **Lesson 10: Problem Solving (cont.)**

On string instruments, placing your finger at different places along the string produces different sound intervals. For example, placing your finger $\frac{3}{4}$ of the string length from the bridge will produce a fourth interval. The chart below is used for numbers 5 and 6, and shows the needed ratio of string length from the bridge to produce the given interval.

INTERVAL	RATIO
third	$\frac{4}{5}$
fourth	$\frac{3}{4}$
fifth	$\frac{2}{3}$
sixth	$\frac{3}{5}$
octave	$\frac{1}{2}$

5. A cello string is 24 in. from the bridge to the scroll. How far from the bridge would you place your finger to produce a fifth interval?

    (A) 20 in.
    (B) 10 in.
    (C) 16 in.
    (D) 14 in.

6. For an instrument with a 10-inch string, where would you place your finger to play a third interval?

    (F) 6 in.
    (G) 8 in.
    (H) 10 in.
    (J) not given

7. Travis and Marty had $45 to spend on gifts for their parents. They both had earned the money, but Travis had earned $5 more than Marty. How much did Marty earn?

    (A) $20
    (B) $25
    (C) $15
    (D) $30

8. Phyllis bought sneakers for $59. The next week, the sneakers went on sale for 25% off. How much would Phyllis have saved if she had waited for the sale?

    (F) $20.00
    (G) $14.25
    (H) $14.75
    (J) $11.50

9. A softball player gets a hit 4 times out of every 11 times she comes to bat. She batted 44 times last season. How many hits did she get?

    (A) 11
    (B) 44
    (C) 4
    (D) 16

10. Which data does not belong?

    (F) 1 hr.
    (G) 60 min.
    (H) 12 in.
    (J) 3600 sec.

1 hr.	60 min.
12 in.	3600 sec.

11. Which data does not belong?

    (A) 123
    (B) 555
    (C) 321
    (D) 231

123	231
555	321

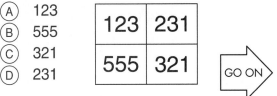

GO ON

MATH: APPLICATIONS

● Lesson 10: Problem Solving (cont.)

12. A grill holds two steaks. What is the shortest time to grill 3 steaks if each side takes 10 minutes to cook?

- (F) 10 minutes
- (G) 20 minutes
- (H) 25 minutes
- (J) 30 minutes

13. The number of water lilies in a pond doubles each day. From the time one lily was placed in a pond until the time the pond was completely covered with lilies took 30 days. After how many days was the pond half covered?

- (A) 15 days
- (B) 16 days
- (C) 29 days
- (D) not enough information

14. Two truckers drove from Dayton to Toledo and back. The first trucker drove to Toledo at 50 mph and returned to Dayton at 60 mph. The second trucker drove to Toledo and back at 57 mph. If the round trip is 300 miles, which driver took longer to make the round trip?

- (F) first trucker
- (G) second trucker
- (H) they both had same amount of time
- (J) not enough information

15. Which of these sampling methods will give the best random sample of 65 students from the entire school population of 650?

- (A) Choose the 65 students in Mr. Green's advanced computer classes.
- (B) Select the first 65 students that walk out the front door of school at the end of the day.
- (C) Choose the 65 students with the highest grade point average.
- (D) Select the 65 oldest children at the school.

16. The table shows the number of students who went to the snack bar after school on the first four days that it was open. If the pattern continues, how many students will go to the snack bar after school on day 5?

Day	Number of Students
1	78
2	89
3	101
4	114
5	

- (F) 125
- (G) 126
- (H) 127
- (J) 128

MATH: APPLICATIONS

● Lesson 11: Algebra

Directions: Find the correct answer to each measurement problem. Mark the space for your choice.

Examples

A. What is the value of y in the number sentence $4y + 3 = 19$?

- (A) 9
- (B) 2
- (C) 3
- (D) 4

B. 36 more than x is 94. Which equation shows this problem?

- (F) $x + 36 = 94$
- (G) $x - 36 = 94$
- (H) $94 \div 36 = x$
- (J) $36 - x = 94$

Clue If you are sure you know which answer is correct, mark the space for your answer and move to the next problem. Before you choose an answer, ask yourself, "Does this answer make sense?"

● Practice

1. What is the missing weight in the balance below?

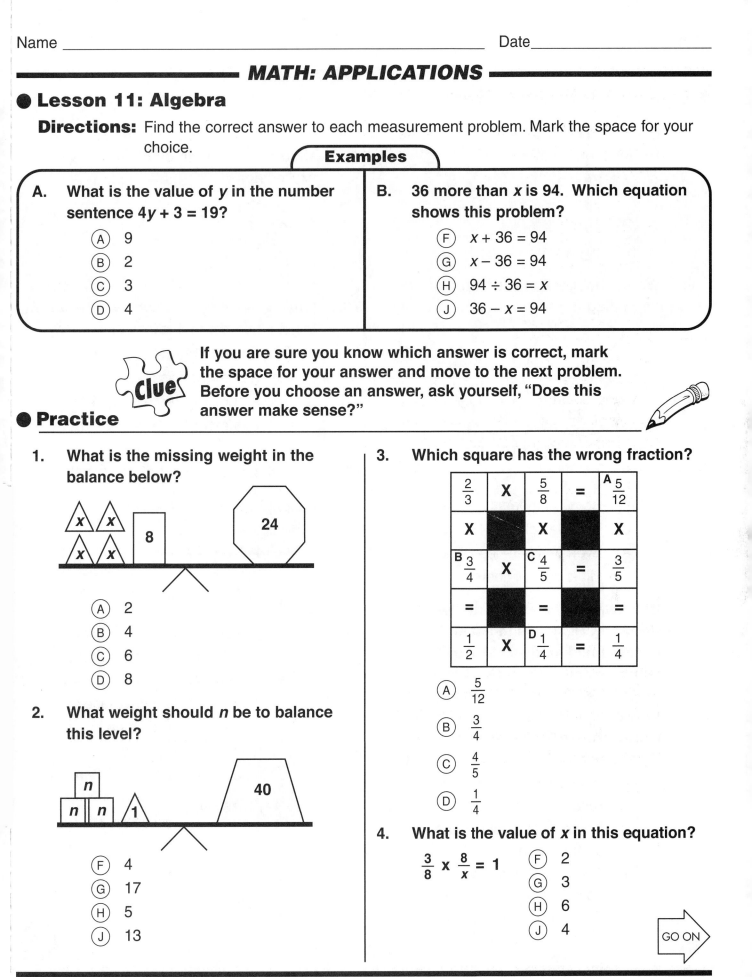

- (A) 2
- (B) 4
- (C) 6
- (D) 8

2. What weight should n be to balance this level?

- (F) 4
- (G) 17
- (H) 5
- (J) 13

3. Which square has the wrong fraction?

- (A) $\frac{5}{12}$
- (B) $\frac{3}{4}$
- (C) $\frac{4}{5}$
- (D) $\frac{1}{4}$

4. What is the value of x in this equation?

$$\frac{3}{8} \times \frac{8}{x} = 1$$

- (F) 2
- (G) 3
- (H) 6
- (J) 4

GO ON

MATH: APPLICATIONS

● Lesson 11: Algebra (cont.)

5. For which of these equations would
    $a = 8$ when $b = 12$?

    (A) $2a - b = 14$

    (B) $2b - a = 22$

    (C) $2a + b = 28$

    (D) $b - a = 10$

6. What label goes in the blank on the
    Venn diagram below?

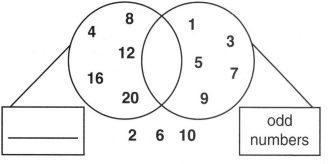

    (F) Prime numbers

    (G) Multiples of 4

    (H) Even numbers less than 30

    (J) Mid-sized numbers

7. **Bob owns a small construction
    company. His job is to estimate the
    cost to build houses. One of the
    equations he uses is $C = A$ x $89.00,
    where A is the area in square feet of
    the house and $89.00 is the average
    cost of construction per square foot.
    What do you think the C stands for?**

    (A) The number of square feet in the
        house

    (B) The cost of finishing each room
        in the house

    (C) The real estate broker's
        commission

    (D) The building cost to the owner

8. If $6 < a$ and $a < b$, what symbol
    should replace the blank in the
    expression b _____ 5?

    (F) <

    (G) =

    (H) >

    (J) –

9. What number must be subtracted from 10
    to get a number that is less than ⁻3?

    (A) a number greater than 13

    (B) a number less than 10

    (C) a number greater than 4

    (D) a number between ⁻3 and 10

10. If $a = 6$ and $b = 12$, what is the value of
    the expression $\frac{(4a + b)}{6} =$

    (F) 5

    (G) 6

    (H) 10

    (J) ⁻2

11. **Suppose that a and b are positive
    numbers and that $a > b$. What is always
    true about the ratio $(a \times 2) \div (b \times 2)$?**

    (A) The ratio is less than one.

    (B) The ratio is more than one.

    (C) The ratio is equal to one.

    (D) The ratio is a negative number.

12. If $3y + 0 = 36$ then $y =$

    (F) 24

    (G) 8

    (H) 12

    (J) 14

STOP

Name _____   Date_____

● **Directions:** Read and work each problem. Fill in the circle that corresponds to your choice.

Examples

A.   Kate bought 6 rolls of film. One roll can take 24 pictures. If Kate takes an average of 12 pictures a week, how long will the film last?

  (A)   6 weeks
  (B)   3 months
  (C)   6 years
  (D)   6 days

B.   What is the area of a warehouse that is 150 feet by 300 feet?

  (F)   40,000 ft.²
  (G)   45,000 ft.²
  (H)   90,000 ft.²
  (J)   100,000 ft.²

1.   Tyler has a great part-time job that requires him to work three 4-hour shifts through the week, and one 8-hour shift on the weekend. How many hours does he work each week?

  (A)   8 hours
  (B)   12 hours
  (C)   20 hours
  (D)   49 hours

2.   Stephanie had a submarine sandwich and a soft drink for $5.28. Alyson ordered the same thing. Jeanie and Angie split a pizza that cost $13.00 and each had a soft drink that cost $1.25. Which of the following would be the closest to a 20% tip on the total purchase?

  (F) $2.00
  (G) $2.50
  (H) $4.00
  (J) $5.00

3.   The Riverwalk Mall has increased its number of stores by 30% in the past 3 years. Three years ago there were 160 stores. How many are there now?

  (A)   160
  (B)   180
  (C)   48
  (D)   208

4.   Which of these angles is less than 90°?

  (F)   ∠ abc
  (G)   ∠ efg
  (H)   ∠ hij
  (J)   ∠ klm

5.   Subtract to find the area of the shaded area.

  (A)   49 in.²
  (B)   24.5 in.²
  (C)   10.5 in.²
  (D)   18.5 in.²

7"
7"

GO ON

6. Ron was given a bag of colored candy pieces and asked to figure some odds. He counted 42 red pieces, 25 yellow pieces, 10 green pieces, and 13 blue pieces. He put all the candy pieces into a jar, stirred them up, and then poured one out of the jar. What were the odds that it was a green one?

    (F) 1 in 4
    (G) 1 in 9
    (H) 1 in 10
    (J) 2 in 5

7. A roll of tape contained 2 meters. If each box required 50 centimeters of tape, how many boxes could be secured with one roll of tape?

    (A) 2
    (B) 4
    (C) 6
    (D) 8

8. Below is a diagram of an expression used by a framing company for determining the number of 1 in. by 1 in. tiles needed to frame a square trivet. The size of the square trivet below is 4 inches on each side. How many tiles are needed to frame it?

    (F) 16
    (G) 20
    (H) 18
    (J) 22

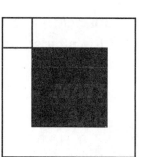

9. A taxi driver works five days a week. This week he drove 268 miles, 242 miles, 310 miles, and 224 miles. What is the average distance he drove this week?

    (A) 228 miles
    (B) 216 miles
    (C) 261 miles
    (D) 284 miles

10. Pamela has a truck that is 1.1 meters long, 0.4 meters high, and 0.7 meters wide. What is the volume of the truck?

    (F) 0.308 m³
    (G) 2.2 m³
    (H) 30.8 m³
    (J) 4.4 m³

11. Two integers have a product of 100, and their sum, when divided in half, equals 26. What are the integers?

    (A) 10 and 10
    (B) 2 and 50
    (C) 5 and 20
    (D) not enough information

12. For which of these equations would $x = 6$ when $y = 12$?

    (F) $x = 3y$
    (G) $x = 2y$
    (H) $x = \frac{1}{2}y$
    (J) $x = \frac{1}{3}y$

GO ON

13. Which of these is the greatest volume?

   (A) 4500 milliliters

   (B) 450 liters

   (C) 450 milliliters

   (D) 45 kiloliters

14. Jamela arrived at the museum at 2:30. Michael arrived 1 hour and 10 minutes later. Alana arrived 25 minutes after Michael. At what time did Alana arrive?

   (F) 2:55

   (G) 3:40

   (H) 4:05

   (J) none of the above

15. A triangle measured 0.75 meters high and 0.4 meters wide at its base. What is the area of the triangle?

   (A) 3 m²

   (B) 0.3 m²

   (C) 1.5 m²

   (D) 0.15 m²

16. What is the circumference of the circle?

5 cm

   (F) 31.4 cm

   (G) 15.7 cm

   (H) 86.3 cm

   (J) none of the above

17. What is the square root of 289?

   (A) 11

   (B) 13

   (C) 17

   (D) 19

18. There are different time zones in the United States. When it is 9:00 P.M. in New York, it is 6:00 P.M. in California. If a plane leaves New York at 8:00 A.M. New York time and lands in California at 11:00 A.M. California time, how long was the flight?

   (F) 2 hours

   (G) 6 hours

   (H) 7 hours

   (J) 8 hours

19. In triangle ABC, angle A measures 45 degrees. Angle B measured 7 degrees more than angle C. What is the measure of angle C?

   (A) 45 degrees

   (B) 71 degrees

   (C) 64 degrees

   (D) not enough information

20. For which of these equations would $a = 5$ when $b = 6$?

   (F) $a - b = 11$

   (G) $a + b = 11$

   (H) $a + b = 1$

   (J) $a - b = 1$

GO ON

MATH: APPLICATIONS
SAMPLE TEST (cont.)

21. A sporting goods store is having a sale on T-shirts. If you buy one T-shirt at regular price, you can buy the second T-shirt at half price. If the regular price of one T-shirt is $11.00, how much would it cost to buy two?

　Ⓐ $11.00
　Ⓑ $22.00
　Ⓒ $16.50
　Ⓓ not enough information

22. Five people attend a dinner party. If every person shakes hands with all the other people at the party, how many handshakes will there be?

　Ⓕ 8
　Ⓖ 12
　Ⓗ 6
　Ⓙ 10

23. Jackie entered the elevator on the floor where her mom is located. She went up 3 floors, down 3 floors, and up 10 floors. She got off the elevator to attend a meeting. After the meeting, she rode the elevator down 9 floors, up 4 floors, and finally down 6 floors to the first floor to eat in the restaurant. On what floor is Jackie's mom?

　Ⓐ 4th floor
　Ⓑ 2nd floor
　Ⓒ 5th floor
　Ⓓ 9th floor

24. What is the area of the shaded portion of the figure below?

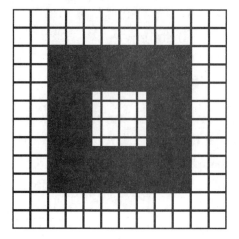

　Ⓕ 55 units
　Ⓖ 144 units
　Ⓗ 89 units
　Ⓙ 40 units

25. In the circle below, the shaded portion represents the percentage of students who passed a fitness test. What percentage of students passed the test?

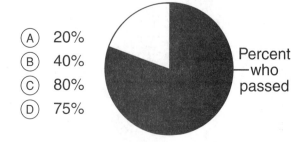

　Ⓐ 20%
　Ⓑ 40%
　Ⓒ 80%
　Ⓓ 75%

Percent who passed

26. A Jaguar XJ220 traveled 217 miles/hour. How many feet/minute was the Jaguar traveling?

　Ⓕ 10,400 ft./min.
　Ⓖ 19,096 ft./min.
　Ⓗ 16,084 ft./min.
　Ⓙ 17,076 ft./min.

ANSWER SHEET

STUDENT'S NAME

LAST · **FIRST** · **MI**

(Bubble grid A–Z for each letter column)

SCHOOL

TEACHER

FEMALE ○   MALE ○

BIRTH DATE

MONTH	DAY	YEAR
JAN ○	0 0	0
FEB ○	1 1	1
MAR ○	2 2	2
APR ○	3 3	3
MAY ○	4	4
JUN ○	5	5 5
JUL ○	6	6 6
AUG ○	7	7 7
SEP ○	8	8 8
OCT ○	9	9 9
NOV ○	0	0
DEC ○		

GRADE

⑦ ⑧ ⑨

Part 1: CONCEPTS

A	Ⓐ Ⓑ Ⓒ Ⓓ	3 Ⓐ Ⓑ Ⓒ Ⓓ	7 Ⓐ Ⓑ Ⓒ Ⓓ	11 Ⓐ Ⓑ Ⓒ Ⓓ	15 Ⓐ Ⓑ Ⓒ Ⓓ
B	Ⓕ Ⓖ Ⓗ Ⓙ	4 Ⓕ Ⓖ Ⓗ Ⓙ	8 Ⓕ Ⓖ Ⓗ Ⓙ	12 Ⓕ Ⓖ Ⓗ Ⓙ	16 Ⓕ Ⓖ Ⓗ Ⓙ
1	Ⓐ Ⓑ Ⓒ Ⓓ	5 Ⓐ Ⓑ Ⓒ Ⓓ	9 Ⓐ Ⓑ Ⓒ Ⓓ	13 Ⓐ Ⓑ Ⓒ Ⓓ	17 Ⓐ Ⓑ Ⓒ Ⓓ
2	Ⓕ Ⓖ Ⓗ Ⓙ	6 Ⓕ Ⓖ Ⓗ Ⓙ	10 Ⓕ Ⓖ Ⓗ Ⓙ	14 Ⓕ Ⓖ Ⓗ Ⓙ	

Part 2: COMPUTATION

A	Ⓐ Ⓑ Ⓒ Ⓓ	3 Ⓐ Ⓑ Ⓒ Ⓓ	7 Ⓐ Ⓑ Ⓒ Ⓓ	11 Ⓐ Ⓑ Ⓒ Ⓓ	15 Ⓐ Ⓑ Ⓒ Ⓓ	19 Ⓐ Ⓑ Ⓒ Ⓓ
B	Ⓕ Ⓖ Ⓗ Ⓙ	4 Ⓕ Ⓖ Ⓗ Ⓙ	8 Ⓕ Ⓖ Ⓗ Ⓙ	12 Ⓕ Ⓖ Ⓗ Ⓙ	16 Ⓕ Ⓖ Ⓗ Ⓙ	20 Ⓕ Ⓖ Ⓗ Ⓙ
1	Ⓐ Ⓑ Ⓒ Ⓓ	5 Ⓐ Ⓑ Ⓒ Ⓓ	9 Ⓐ Ⓑ Ⓒ Ⓓ	13 Ⓐ Ⓑ Ⓒ Ⓓ	17 Ⓐ Ⓑ Ⓒ Ⓓ	21 Ⓐ Ⓑ Ⓒ Ⓓ
2	Ⓕ Ⓖ Ⓗ Ⓙ	6 Ⓕ Ⓖ Ⓗ Ⓙ	10 Ⓕ Ⓖ Ⓗ Ⓙ	14 Ⓕ Ⓖ Ⓗ Ⓙ	18 Ⓕ Ⓖ Ⓗ Ⓙ	22 Ⓕ Ⓖ Ⓗ Ⓙ

Part 3: APPLICATIONS

A	Ⓐ Ⓑ Ⓒ Ⓓ	3 Ⓐ Ⓑ Ⓒ Ⓓ	7 Ⓐ Ⓑ Ⓒ Ⓓ	11 Ⓐ Ⓑ Ⓒ Ⓓ	15 Ⓐ Ⓑ Ⓒ Ⓓ
B	Ⓕ Ⓖ Ⓗ Ⓙ	4 Ⓕ Ⓖ Ⓗ Ⓙ	8 Ⓕ Ⓖ Ⓗ Ⓙ	12 Ⓕ Ⓖ Ⓗ Ⓙ	16 Ⓕ Ⓖ Ⓗ Ⓙ
1	Ⓐ Ⓑ Ⓒ Ⓓ	5 Ⓐ Ⓑ Ⓒ Ⓓ	9 Ⓐ Ⓑ Ⓒ Ⓓ	13 Ⓐ Ⓑ Ⓒ Ⓓ	
2	Ⓕ Ⓖ Ⓗ Ⓙ	6 Ⓕ Ⓖ Ⓗ Ⓙ	10 Ⓕ Ⓖ Ⓗ Ⓙ	14 Ⓕ Ⓖ Ⓗ Ⓙ	

MATH: PRACTICE TEST

● Part 1: Concepts

Directions: Read and work each problem. Fill in the circle that corresponds to your choice.

Examples

A. Which of these decimals is equal to $\frac{3}{8}$?
- (A) 0.375
- (B) 0.78
- (C) 0.37
- (D) 0.0375

B. Of these choices, which is the smallest number that can be divided evenly by 6 and 36?
- (F) 108
- (G) 6
- (H) 54
- (J) 72

1. $\sqrt{169}$
- (A) 12
- (B) 11
- (C) 13
- (D) 14

2. The distance from Nogales to Tucson is 92 miles. From Tucson to Phoenix is 110 miles. Which numbers would you use to estimate the distance from Nogales to Phoenix by going through Tucson?
- (F) 90 and 110
- (G) 100 and 100
- (H) 120 and 110
- (J) 80 and 100

3. What is the prime factorization of 72?
- (A) 2 x 2 x 2 x 3 x 3
- (B) 6 x 6 x 2
- (C) 2 x 3 x 2 x 6
- (D) 36 x 2

4. What should replace the blank space in the number sentence below?

   0.0043 x _____ = 43
- (F) 10^{-4}
- (G) 10^3
- (H) 10^4
- (J) 10^5

5. Which number sentence is true?
- (A) 2 < 0
- (B) ⁻4 > 2
- (C) 3 > ⁻1
- (D) ⁻3 < ⁻13

6. How much would the value of 364,921 increase by replacing the 3 with a 5?
- (F) 200,000
- (G) 2,000
- (H) 20,000
- (J) 200

7. Which arrow points most closely to $-\frac{3}{8}$?

- (A) M
- (B) N
- (C) O
- (D) P

GO ON

MATH: PRACTICE TEST
Part 1: Concepts (cont.)

8. $\frac{5}{9} = \frac{20}{x}$

    $x =$ _____

    (F) 9
    (G) 36
    (H) 24
    (J) 15

9. Which of these is 8,425,376 rounded to the nearest hundred thousand?

    (A) 8,430,000
    (B) 8,425,000
    (C) 8,400,000
    (D) 8,425,400

10. $9^4 =$ _____

    (F) 9 x 4
    (G) 9 x 9
    (H) 9 x 9 x 9
    (J) 9 x 9 x 9 x 9

11. What number completes the number sentence below?

    13 x □ = 26 x 20

    (A) 18
    (B) 40
    (C) 26
    (D) 5

12. Which is the best estimate

    of $21\frac{1}{5}$ x 9.84?

    (F) 21 x 7
    (G) 21 x 10
    (H) 20 x 10
    (J) 20 x 5

13. What is the reciprocal of $\frac{2}{9}$?

    (A) $\frac{9}{2}$
    (B) 9 x 2
    (C) 2 x 9
    (D) 1

14. $15.18 \times 10^4 =$ _____

    (F) 0.1518
    (G) 1.5118
    (H) 1578
    (J) 151,800

15. Which of these is greater than the others?

    (A) one fourth
    (B) one and one eighth
    (C) one and three tenths
    (D) one and four hundredths

16. What is the value of the expression $(12 - 3)^2 \div 9$?

    (F) 81
    (G) 27
    (H) 18
    (J) 9

17. How would you write 37% as a fraction?

    (A) 0.37
    (B) $\frac{37}{100}$
    (C) $\frac{3}{7}$
    (D) $\frac{7}{3}$

STOP

Name _____   Date_____

● **Part 2: Computation**

Directions: Find the correct answer for each problem. Mark the space for your choice. Choose "none of these" if the correct answer is not given.

Examples

A. $^-4 \times ^-9 =$
- (A) 13
- (B) 18
- (C) 36
- (D) $^-13$

B. $\frac{1}{3} \div 3 =$
- (F) $\frac{1}{9}$
- (G) 9
- (H) $\frac{1}{6}$
- (J) 6

1. $^-50 \times ^-6 =$
- (A) $^-300$
- (B) 300
- (C) $^-56$
- (D) 56

2. $9\frac{5}{6}$
  $-\ \frac{7}{12}$
- (F) $9\frac{1}{4}$
- (G) $8\frac{1}{4}$
- (H) $9\frac{1}{3}$
- (J) $9\frac{1}{2}$

3. $0.042 \div 62 =$
- (A) 0.7
- (B) 0.007
- (C) 0.0007
- (D) 0.07

4. 30% of □ = 24
- (F) 21
- (G) 72
- (H) 80
- (J) 720

5. $\frac{3}{8} \times \frac{2}{3} =$
- (A) $\frac{4}{8}$
- (B) $\frac{1}{4}$
- (C) $\frac{6}{20}$
- (D) $\frac{1}{8}$

6. $\begin{array}{r} 494 \\ -\ 37 \end{array}$
- (F) 531
- (G) 412
- (H) 487
- (J) 457

7. $0.7\overline{)567}$
- (A) 77
- (B) 870
- (C) 810
- (D) 880

8. $\begin{array}{r} 0.816 \\ \times\ 0.456 \end{array}$
- (F) 0.472034
- (G) 0.370094
- (H) 0.372096
- (J) 0.352375

9. $\begin{array}{r} \frac{13}{16} \\ -\ \frac{9}{16} \end{array}$
- (A) $\frac{1}{2}$
- (B) $\frac{1}{4}$
- (C) $\frac{1}{3}$
- (D) $\frac{1}{8}$

10. $56 - 18 \times 2 \div 4 =$
- (F) 19
- (G) 16
- (H) 5
- (J) 47

GO ON

11. $\frac{3}{4} \div \frac{5}{8} =$
   - (A) $1\frac{1}{5}$
   - (B) 2
   - (C) $\frac{3}{4}$
   - (D) $1\frac{1}{8}$

12. **23.4 is 30% of what number?**
   - (F) 68
   - (G) 140
   - (H) 88
   - (J) 78

13. $(86 - 79)(8 \div 7) =$
   - (A) 12
   - (B) 9.6
   - (C) 8.0
   - (D) 81

14. $\frac{^-96}{^-12}$
   - (F) 8
   - (G) $^-8$
   - (H) $^-18$
   - (J) 18

15. $\frac{17}{20}$
    $+ \frac{13}{20}$
   - (A) 11
   - (B) $1\frac{1}{2}$
   - (C) 101
   - (D) none of these

16. $3\frac{1}{8} \times \frac{3}{7} =$
   - (F) $2\frac{15}{56}$
   - (G) $3\frac{1}{5}$
   - (H) $4\frac{1}{28}$
   - (J) none of these

17. $\frac{(95 + 5) - 10}{5}$
   - (A) 18
   - (B) 85
   - (C) 10
   - (D) none of these

18. $^-43 + ^-9 =$
   - (F) 34
   - (G) $^-52$
   - (H) $^-34$
   - (J) 52

19. $\frac{9}{10} \times \frac{14}{100} =$
   - (A) 0.126
   - (B) 0.0126
   - (C) 0.8116
   - (D) 0.08116

20.
$$6.216\overline{)803.7288}$$
   - (F) 1.293
   - (G) 12.93
   - (H) 129.3
   - (J) 1293

21. $6\frac{2}{3} + 8\frac{5}{6} =$
   - (A) $17\frac{1}{2}$
   - (B) $21\frac{2}{3}$
   - (C) 24
   - (D) none of these

22. $(16.3 + 0.027) \div 5.21 =$
   - (F) 3.323
   - (G) 3.186
   - (H) 3.147
   - (J) 3.134

STOP

MATH: PRACTICE TEST

● Part 3: Applications

Directions: Read and work each problem. Fill in the circle that corresponds to your choice.

Examples

A. If $2x - 12 = 14$, then $x =$
- (A) 4
- (B) 26
- (C) 16
- (D) 13

B. Molly had a gallon of milk. If she drank a pint, how many cups of milk were left in the container?
- (F) 4 cups
- (G) 3 cups
- (H) 6 cups
- (J) 14 cups

---

1. There are 24 windows in a house. Each window has 2 panes of glass. If it takes 3 minutes to clean one pane, how long will it take to clean all the windows?
- (A) 98 minutes
- (B) 2 hrs. 24 minutes
- (C) 72 minutes
- (D) 1 hour

2. Reba has $750.00 in her bank account. The account earns 3% interest a year. Which equation will tell us how much money will be in the savings account at the end of the year?
- (F) 750 x .03 =
- (G) 750 + (750 x .03) =
- (H) 750 ÷ (.03 x 750) =
- (J) 750 x .03 + .04 =

3. The gas tank in a car holds 22 gallons. It is now half full. If gas costs $1.39 a gallon, which equation will tell us how much will it cost to fill the tank?
- (A) $22 \times \frac{1}{2} + 1.39 =$
- (B) $1.39 \times (22 \times \frac{1}{2}) =$
- (C) $1.39 \times (22 + \frac{1}{2}) =$
- (D) none of the above

4. What is the median of the following set of numbers? **(4, 2, 3, 3, 3, 6)**
- (F) 2
- (G) 3
- (H) 4
- (J) 3.5

5. For which of these equations would $a = 9$ when $b = 6$?
- (A) $3a - 21 = b$
- (B) $2b - a = {}^-4$
- (C) $2a - 9 = b$
- (D) $4a - 2b = 18$

6. 12.3 liters is the same as—
- (F) 123 milliliters
- (G) 12.3 milliliters
- (H) 12,300 milliliters
- (J) 1,230 milliliters

7. What is the area of the region shaded below?
- (A) 9.42 ft.²
- (B) 4.54 ft.²
- (C) 3.192 ft.²
- (D) 2.43 ft.²

GO ON

MATH: PRACTICE TEST
Part 3: Applications (cont.)

8. The two soft drink bottles are—

- (F) neither congruent nor similar.
- (G) congruent but not similar.
- (H) similar but not congruent.
- (J) similar and congruent.

9. You take out a loan for $200 with an annual interest rate of 10%. If you make no payments, how long would it take to acquire $66.20 in interest?

- (A) $2 \frac{1}{2}$ yrs.
- (B) 2 yrs.
- (C) 3 yrs.
- (D) 4 yrs.

10. You flip a coin 150 times. What is the probability of getting tails on any one flip?

- (F) 1 in 3
- (G) 1 in 2
- (H) 1 in 4
- (J) 1 in 10

11. A sheet of copy paper measures about—

- (A) 3 in. by 4 in.
- (B) 4 in. by 8 in.
- (C) 8 in. by 11 in.
- (D) 12 in. by 16 in.

12. In the triangle below, angle ABC is a right angle. If angle BAC equals 60°, what is the measure of angle ACB?

- (F) 30°
- (G) 45°
- (H) 60°
- (J) 90°

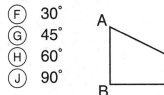

13. What is the total interest earned?

principal	annual rate	time	interest
$100.00	7%	3 years	

- (A) $21.00
- (B) $22.50
- (C) $31.00
- (D) $32.50

14. What fraction of 6 gallons is 6 pints?

- (F) $\frac{1}{48}$
- (G) $\frac{1}{8}$
- (H) $\frac{3}{16}$
- (J) none of these

15. For which of these equations would $a = 5$ when $b = 3$?

- (A) $ab = 12$
- (B) $a^2 = b^2 + 3$
- (C) $2a + b = 13$
- (D) $3a = b + 2$

16. At a family reunion in the Southwest, there were 24 people from California, 18 from New Mexico, and 8 from Arizona. If you began speaking to 1 of the people without knowing where the person was from, what are the chances the person would be from California?

- (F) 1 out of 2
- (G) 24 out of 26
- (H) 12 out of 25
- (J) none of the above

STOP

SCIENCE

● Lesson 1: General Knowledge

Directions: Read each question. Mark the answer you think is correct.

Example

A. A metal that is made of a mixture of different metals is called—

- (A) gold.
- (B) compound.
- (C) alloy.
- (D) soft metal.

1. Which of the following would you do first if you wanted to set up your own science experiment?

- (A) Gather the necessary materials.
- (B) Make a hypothesis.
- (C) Examine your data.
- (D) Predict what will happen in the experiment.

2. A positively charged particle, found within the nucleus of an atom is called—

- (F) a proton.
- (G) a neutron.
- (H) an electron.
- (J) a chloroplast.

3. Which of the following is not one of the states of matter?

- (A) gas
- (B) compound
- (C) solid
- (D) liquid

4. Microwaves can cook food in a fraction of the time because—

- (F) they use a lot of power.
- (G) they get into the middle of the food and make the molecules in the food vibrate quickly.
- (H) they make the food taste better.
- (J) their spinning rotation helps to make the food pass over the cooking element much faster.

5. The gas that sometimes makes some soft drinks fizz is—

- (A) oxygen.
- (B) hydrogen.
- (C) carbon dioxide.
- (D) carbon monoxide.

6. An educated guess, that can be tested, about how an experiment will turn out is called—

- (F) a conclusion.
- (G) a prediction.
- (H) a hypothesis.
- (J) an observation.

GO ON

Name _____   Date_____

SCIENCE

● Lesson 1: General Knowledge (cont.)

7. The central part of a plant or animal cell is called the—
   - (A) atom.
   - (B) cell wall.
   - (C) chlorophyll.
   - (D) nucleus.

8. The chemical symbol for pure hydrogen is—
   - (F) H_2O
   - (G) Hg
   - (H) H
   - (J) H_2

9. What type of graph would be best to compare the atomic weights of different elements?
   - (A) a pie chart
   - (B) a multiple-line graph
   - (C) a Venn diagram
   - (D) a bar graph

10. The temperature at which a heated liquid turns to a gas is called its—
    - (F) boiling point.
    - (G) vapor point.
    - (H) freezing point.
    - (J) atomic temperature.

11. Kyla's frozen pop has turned into liquid. The frozen pop has reached its—
    - (A) freezing point.
    - (B) melting point.
    - (C) point of no return.
    - (D) boiling point.

12. The most abundant element on Earth is—
    - (F) oxygen.
    - (G) nitrogen.
    - (H) hydrogen.
    - (J) carbon.

13. In outer space, an astronaut floats because the pull of Earth's _____ is weaker.
    - (A) attraction
    - (B) velocity
    - (C) weight
    - (D) gravity

14. Which of the following would you not find in an atom?
    - (F) protons
    - (G) cytoplasm
    - (H) neutrons
    - (J) nucleus

15. The chemical symbol for steam is—
    - (A) HO_2
    - (B) HO
    - (C) H_2O
    - (D) O_2H

16. Which of the following does not orbit the sun?
    - (F) Mercury
    - (G) the moon
    - (H) Pluto
    - (J) Earth

17. When sugar is added to water, which of the following is formed?
    - (A) compound
    - (B) solution
    - (C) element
    - (D) gas

GO ON

SCIENCE

● Lesson 1: General Knowledge (cont.)

18. **Batteries work as a source of power because—**

    (F) they can be made to last forever.

    (G) they provide an electric force that pushes electrons around a circuit.

    (H) batteries come in different sizes to accommodate various needs.

    (J) hooking them up to whatever it is they power is very simple.

19. **Which of the following is not a type of rock?**

    (A) igneous

    (B) sedimentary

    (C) metamorphic

    (D) chrysalis

20. **Fe is the symbol of what element?**

    (F) tin

    (G) fluorine

    (H) iron

    (J) fermium

21. **Astronomer is to comet as botanist is to _____.**

    (A) geode

    (B) human

    (C) fossil

    (D) plant

22. **You decide to measure how the volume of a sample of salt water changes over time. You will use a _____ to measure the change in volume.**

    (F) digital scale

    (G) beaker

    (H) tape measure

    (J) graduated cylinder

23. **You leave the salt water sample in an open container at room temperature for several days. You suspect that some of the water from the mixture will—**

    (A) crystallize.

    (B) expand.

    (C) condense.

    (D) evaporate.

24. **At the end of this experiment, you see that the volume of the salt water has decreased. The law of conservation of matter helps you to conclude that—**

    (F) some of the water disappeared forever.

    (G) the "missing" water has not really disappeared, but it has changed form.

    (H) the salt was absorbed the water.

    (J) salt water has a much lower freezing point than fresh water.

25. **In this experiment, the salt water is an example of—**

    (A) a solute.

    (B) a compound.

    (C) an element.

    (D) a mixture.

26. **Icy roads are slippery because—**

    (F) there is very little friction.

    (G) the extra molecules in cold water make it very slippery.

    (H) drivers are easily intimidated.

    (J) icy water runs downhill.

STOP

■ SCIENCE ■

● Lesson 2: Reading and Understanding

Directions: Read the passage and then read the questions. Mark the answers you think are correct.

Lightning Strikes

Lightning contains an enormous amount of electricity. One bolt of lightning contains enough electric energy to supply the power for one small town for one year! Lightning starts inside a cloud where air currents toss ice crystals and water droplets around so hard that they knock the electrons off one another's atoms as they collide. The droplets that lose the electrons become positively charged. The extra electrons fall to the bottom of the cloud and accumulate, building up a charge, or electrical potential, of about 300,000 volts per foot. Lightning neutralizes this charge by allowing the electrons to flow back positively charged droplets of crystals.

If two adjacent clouds have opposite charges, the lightning jumps from cloud to cloud. If not, the lightning jumps from a cloud to the ground. Lightning always seeks the best conductor to reach the ground, such as a lightning rod, a tall building, or a tall tree.

1. **Lightning moves from one cloud to another when—**
   - (A) both clouds have the same charge.
   - (B) both clouds have opposite charges.
   - (C) the clouds come into contact with another.
   - (D) clouds develop strange shapes.

2. **The cause of lightning can best be explained by—**
   - (F) white light that comes to the ground.
   - (G) a collection of extra protons near the bottom of the cloud.
   - (H) a collection of extra electrons at the bottom of a cloud.
   - (J) Mother Nature's Revenge.

3. **Lightning comes to the ground when—**
   - (A) there is enough moisture in the air to bring the charge to earth.
   - (B) a good target is spotted.
   - (C) clouds become saturated with water.
   - (D) there are no nearby clouds with an opposite charge.

4. **Hundreds of people are struck by lightning every year. Which of the following is probably the best place to be during an electrical storm?**
   - (F) on a golf course
   - (G) under a tall tree
   - (H) in an open field
   - (J) inside a building

SCIENCE

● Lesson 3: Reading and Understanding

Directions: Read the passage and then read each question. Mark the answers you think are correct.

The Electric Eel

Several species of fish produce electric impulses that they can pass into the surrounding water. The electric eel, which can grow to a length of ten feet, is one of the most astonishing. The electric impulse from an electric eel can measure as high as 650 volts of electricity, equivalent to 50 car batteries. This is enough to stun or kill its prey and give a severe shock to a man or large animal. Interestingly, these eels are born with normal eyesight but become blind as they grow older.

The organs which produce electricity in the eel consist of electroplates that line each side of the tail. These organs contain thousands of tiny electroplates and compose almost half of the body weight of the eel. While the eel is resting at the bottom of the sea, it does not emit electric impulses. As it starts to swim about, it emits low-voltage electric discharges which help it locate its prey. The eel prefers to dine on living victims and adjusts the electric discharge from its electroplates to match the size of its prey so that the animal is stunned but not killed.

1. **How is the impulse that is emitted by an eel produced?**

    _____

    _____

    _____

2. **Explain in a sentence the main use of the electronic impulses that are produced by the eel.**

    _____

    _____

    _____

    _____

3. **What effect would the discharge of an eel have on a human being?**

    _____

    _____

    _____

Name _____ Date_____

SCIENCE
SAMPLE TEST

● **Directions:** Read each question. Mark the answer you think is correct.

Examples

A. The outside of a cell is called—

(A) the membrane.

(B) the nucleus.

(C) the cytoplasm.

(D) the chloroplast.

B. The layer of gas that protects the Earth from the sun's ultraviolet radiation is called—

(F) radiation.

(G) sunbelt.

(H) atmosphere.

(J) ozone.

---

1. Which instrument would help you calculate the velocity of a human?

(A) a thermometer

(B) a microscope

(C) a barometer

(D) a stopwatch

2. Which planet is smallest and coldest?

(F) Jupiter

(G) Pluto

(H) Earth

(J) Venus

3. The temperature at which, when heated, a substance changes from solid to liquid is called its—

(A) boiling point.

(B) freezing point.

(C) liquefying point.

(D) melting point.

4. All are primary colors except—

(F) red.

(G) green.

(H) blue.

(J) yellow.

5. What is the term for a piece of a meteor that reaches the earth's surface before burning up?

(A) a meteorite

(B) an asteroid

(C) a comet

(D) a UFO

6. H is the symbol of what element?

(F) helium

(G) holmium

(H) hafnium

(J) hydrogen

7. Air pressure is measured with a—

(A) thermometer.

(B) barometer.

(C) hydrometer.

(D) altimeter.

8. The measuring standard for level of noise is—

(F) decibel.

(G) watt.

(H) ohm.

(J) voltage.

GO ON

9. CO_2 is composed of what elements?
   - (A) calcium and oxygen
   - (B) carbon
   - (C) carbon and oxygen
   - (D) carbon dioxide

10. To measure the amount of gas produced by a chemical reaction, the most exact method to use would be—
    - (F) observation.
    - (G) barometric pressure.
    - (H) heating and cooling it.
    - (J) water displacement.

11. The furthest planet from the sun is—
    - (A) Mercury.
    - (B) Saturn.
    - (C) Pluto.
    - (D) Uranus.

12. The closest planet to the sun is
    - (F) Mars.
    - (G) Earth.
    - (H) Venus.
    - (J) Mercury.

13. Through his telescope, Oscar spies a heavenly body with a long tail of light. Oscar is looking at—
    - (A) an asteroid.
    - (B) the moon.
    - (C) a comet.
    - (D) a speck on the lens of his telescope.

14. A particle with a negative charge is called—
    - (F) a proton.
    - (G) an electron.
    - (H) a neutron.
    - (J) a molecule.

15. A system that uses the echoes of ultrasound waves to detect things that are underwater is called—
    - (A) zone locating.
    - (B) sonar.
    - (C) plankton.
    - (D) deep sea periscope.

16. Sita boils a kettle of water. Some of the water has turned into steam. Sita's water has undergone a—
    - (F) chemical change.
    - (G) melting point.
    - (H) change of scenery.
    - (J) physical change.

17. Hydrogen, helium, and oxygen are all
    - (A) elements.
    - (B) atomic weights.
    - (C) protons.
    - (D) neutrons.

18. A large ball of rock or gas which orbits a star and reflects the star's light but does not give out light of its own is called a—
    - (F) star.
    - (G) planet.
    - (H) comet.
    - (J) meteorite.

STOP

STUDENT'S NAME		SCHOOL

LAST FIRST MI

TEACHER

FEMALE ○   MALE ○

BIRTH DATE

MONTH	DAY	YEAR

JAN ○
FEB ○
MAR ○
APR ○
MAY ○
JUN ○
JUL ○
AUG ○
SEP ○
OCT ○
NOV ○
DEC ○

GRADE

(7) (8) (9)

Part 1: SCIENCE

A	Ⓐ Ⓑ Ⓒ Ⓓ	5	Ⓐ Ⓑ Ⓒ Ⓓ	10	Ⓕ Ⓖ Ⓗ Ⓙ
1	Ⓐ Ⓑ Ⓒ Ⓓ	6	Ⓕ Ⓖ Ⓗ Ⓙ	11	Ⓐ Ⓑ Ⓒ Ⓓ
2	Ⓕ Ⓖ Ⓗ Ⓙ	7	Ⓐ Ⓑ Ⓒ Ⓓ	12	Ⓕ Ⓖ Ⓗ Ⓙ
3	Ⓐ Ⓑ Ⓒ Ⓓ	8	Ⓕ Ⓖ Ⓗ Ⓙ	13	Ⓐ Ⓑ Ⓒ Ⓓ
4	Ⓕ Ⓖ Ⓗ Ⓙ	9	Ⓐ Ⓑ Ⓒ Ⓓ	14	Ⓕ Ⓖ Ⓗ Ⓙ

Name _____ Date _____

SCIENCE PRACTICE TEST

Directions: Find the correct answer to each question. Mark the space that corresponds to your choice.

Example

A. Which of these planets is closest to Earth?
- (A) Venus
- (B) Mercury
- (C) Jupiter
- (D) Saturn

1. The central part of the atom is the—
- (A) proton.
- (B) electron.
- (C) nucleus.
- (D) neutron.

2. What are the colors called that make up white light?
- (F) rainbow
- (G) spectrum
- (H) prism
- (J) pitch

3. Electricity is produced by all of the following except—
- (A) oil and coal.
- (B) water.
- (C) solar cells.
- (D) wood.

4. The speed of jets traveling faster than the speed of sound is measured by a unit called—
- (F) mach.
- (G) erg.
- (H) miles per hour.
- (J) hertz.

5. Friction can be reduced by using—
- (A) an energizing battery.
- (B) a lubricant.
- (C) warm moist air.
- (D) smooth stones.

6. Which of these inventors is credited with developing the first radio transmitter?
- (F) Thomas Edison
- (G) Guglielmo Marconi
- (H) Frank Lloyd Wright
- (J) Oliver Lodge

7. Which of these ocean dwellers is a mammal?
- (A) shark
- (B) tuna
- (C) dolphin
- (D) eel

8. The change of a vapor to a liquid is called—
- (F) condensation.
- (G) evaporation.
- (H) assimilation.
- (J) osmosis.

GO ON

1-57768-978-X *Spectrum Test Practice 8*

Name _____ Date_____

9. The speed at which an object is moving in a particular direction is called—
   - (A) thrust.
   - (B) vibration.
   - (C) velocity.
   - (D) mass.

10. The tendency of objects to remain in motion at the same speed in the same straight line, unless acted on by an outside force is called—
   - (F) inertia.
   - (G) forward progress.
   - (H) friction resistant.
   - (J) viscosity.

11. Which is not part of the eye?
   - (A) iris
   - (B) retina
   - (C) stirrup
   - (D) cornea

12. Your respiratory system includes all of the following except—
   - (F) lungs.
   - (G) trachea.
   - (H) bronchial tube.
   - (J) aorta.

13. The shell is to turtle as _____ is to a skunk.
   - (A) white striping on the back
   - (B) offensive odor
   - (C) camouflage
   - (D) sharp quills

14. Our seasons are caused by—
   - (F) strong winds from the north.
   - (G) the tilt of the earth on its axis.
   - (H) the jet stream.
   - (J) changes in currents near the equator.

Read the passage carefully. Then answer questions 15 and 16 in a sentence or two.

How Are Animals Different?

How are animals different from other living things? What is the difference between an animal and a plant? Between an animal and a bacteria? For one thing, animals show symmetry; their bodies have matching sides. Sometimes an animal has radial symmetry—where the animal has matching parts if you cut it from top to bottom and the parts radiate from the center like spokes from a wheel. (But it does not have a matching right and left side.) Sometimes it has bilateral symmetry—where it matches side to side (the left side is the same as the right side).

15. Explain in a sentence how animals with bilateral symmetry differ from those with radial symmetry.

_____

16. Give examples of why humans are said to have bilateral symmetry.

_____

STOP

SOCIAL STUDIES

● Lesson 1: General Knowledge

Directions: Read each of the following carefully. Then mark the letter that corresponds to the correct answer.

Examples

A. **He wrote our national anthem.**
- (A) Stephen Foster
- (B) Irving Berlin
- (C) James Madison
- (D) Francis Scott Key

B. **He was the only president ever elected unanimously by the Electoral College.**
- (F) George Washington
- (G) Abraham Lincoln
- (H) George W. Bush
- (J) Thomas Jefferson

1. **What is the capital city of Colorado?**
- (A) Colorado Springs
- (B) Denver
- (C) Grand Junction
- (D) Fort Collins

2. **It's sometimes called "Ole Man River."**
- (F) The Missouri River
- (G) The Hudson River
- (H) The Mississippi River
- (J) The Columbia River

3. **Which state does not border Mexico?**
- (A) Arizona
- (B) California
- (C) Texas
- (D) Louisiana

4. **Old Faithful is a—**
- (F) volcano.
- (G) geyser.
- (H) mountain.
- (J) river.

5. **The Green Mountains are located here.**
- (A) Vermont
- (B) Colorado
- (C) New Hampshire
- (D) Wyoming

6. **Who was the only man to be both president and vice president without ever facing the test of an election?**
- (F) Nelson Rockefeller
- (G) Gerald R. Ford
- (H) Lyndon B. Johnson
- (J) William Howard Taft

7. **Which county was not one of the Axis powers during World War II?**
- (A) Germany
- (B) Japan
- (C) Italy
- (D) Soviet Union

8. **The dividing line between the northern and southern hemispheres is—**
- (F) the equator.
- (G) the Tropic of Capricorn.
- (H) the Tropic of Cancer.
- (J) the Atlantic Ocean.

9. **What is the state capital of Illinois?**
- (A) Springfield
- (B) Chicago
- (C) Champaign
- (D) Rockford

GO ON

SOCIAL STUDIES

● Lesson 1: General Knowledge (cont.)

10. Which of these metropolitan areas is largest?

- (F) Chicago
- (G) Los Angeles
- (H) San Francisco
- (J) Detroit

11. In which building was the U.S. Constitution drafted?

- (A) Smithsonian
- (B) Independence Hall
- (C) Freedom Hall
- (D) the White House

12. The Statue of Liberty was a gift to the United States from—

- (F) Great Britain.
- (G) Switzerland.
- (H) Canada.
- (J) France.

13. He was the first to sign the Declaration of Independence.

- (A) Thomas Jefferson
- (B) James Madison
- (C) John Hancock
- (D) Benjamin Franklin

14. Which was the first state to secede from the Union during the Civil War?

- (F) South Carolina
- (G) Tennessee
- (H) Missouri
- (J) Kansas

15. Which of these presidents is not immortalized on Mount Rushmore?

- (A) Abraham Lincoln
- (B) Thomas Jefferson
- (C) Theodore Roosevelt
- (D) John F. Kennedy

16. This state lies between Minnesota and Iowa on the west and Lake Michigan on the east.

- (F) Illinois
- (G) Wisconsin
- (H) Indiana
- (J) Ohio

17. Plymouth, Massachusetts was founded in 1620 by this group of people.

- (A) Amish
- (B) Shakers
- (C) Pilgrims
- (D) Catholics

18. He was both the 22nd and 24th U.S. President.

- (F) Franklin D. Roosevelt
- (G) Dwight D. Eisenhower
- (H) Grover Cleveland
- (J) Jimmy Carter

19. To the north of this state lie Colorado and Kansas; to the south is Texas.

- (A) Oklahoma
- (B) Louisiana
- (C) New Mexico
- (D) Wyoming

STOP

SOCIAL STUDIES

● Lesson 2: Reading and Understanding

Directions: Study the time line that shows important events in the development of transportation in the United States. Then answer questions 1–5.

Transportation in the United States

Robert Fulton's steam-powered boat, the *Clermont*, makes a round trip between Albany and New York in five days.

More than 30,000 miles of railroad track connect towns across the U.S.

The first refrigerator cars are used to keep produce fresh during transport.

The first successful turnpike (tollroad) opens.

The Erie Canal is completed.

The United States has developed more than 3,000 miles of canals and 3,000 miles of railroad track.

Illinois passes the first Granger laws to regulate railroads.

Autos powered by gasoline are invented.

| 1794 | 1807 | 1825 | 1840 | 1860 | 1869 | 1870s | 1892 |

1. **How many years passed between the time the U.S. developed 3,000 miles of railroad track and 30,000 miles of railroad track?**
   - (A) 10 years
   - (B) 2 decades
   - (C) half of a century
   - (D) These events happened during the same year.

2. **When did Illinois pass the first Granger law?**
   - (F) after the Clermont sailed
   - (G) before the Erie Canal was completed
   - (H) during the eighteenth century
   - (J) at the same time as refrigerator cars rolled across the country

3. **During which year is a transportation milestone not related to land travel listed?**
   - (A) 1794
   - (B) 1825
   - (C) 1860
   - (D) 1869

4. **How many years after 3,000 miles of track had been laid did Illinois pass a law to regulate railroads?**
   - (F) 9 years
   - (G) 29 years
   - (H) 49 years
   - (J) 59 years

5. **Which happened earliest?**
   - (A) Autos chugged across the country.
   - (B) Illinois passed a law to regulate railroads.
   - (C) Robert Fulton's boat sailed.
   - (D) The U.S. laid more than 3,000 miles of railroad track.

Name _____   Date_____

═══════════════════════ **SOCIAL STUDIES** ═══════════════════════

● **Lesson 3: Reading and Understanding**

Directions: Study the U.S. map. Then answer questions 1–6.

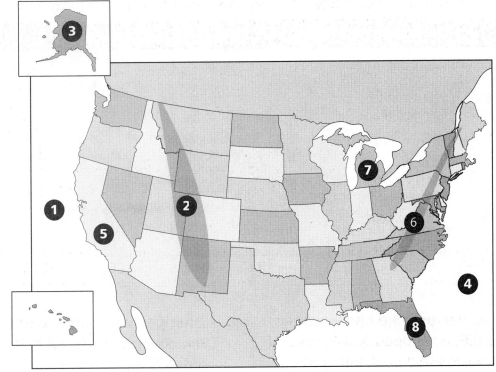

1. **What is the feature labeled 1 on the map?**
   - (A) Atlantic Ocean
   - (B) Gulf of Mexico
   - (C) Pacific Ocean
   - (D) Lake Superior

2. **What is the feature labeled 4 on the map?**
   - (F) Atlantic Ocean
   - (G) Gulf of Mexico
   - (H) Pacific Ocean
   - (J) Lake Superior

3. **What is the feature labeled 5 on the map?**
   - (A) Arizona
   - (B) California
   - (C) Wyoming
   - (D) Texas

4. **What is the feature labeled 8 on the map?**
   - (F) Florida
   - (G) Mississippi
   - (H) South Carolina
   - (J) Miami

5. **What is the feature labeled 2 on the map?**
   - (A) Arizona and New Mexico
   - (B) Rocky Mountains
   - (C) Mississippi Basin
   - (D) Adirondack Mountains

6. **What is the feature labeled 3 on the map?**
   - (F) Hawaiian Islands
   - (G) Arctic Circle
   - (H) Alaska
   - (J) Washington Peninsula

STOP

SOCIAL STUDIES

● Lesson 4: Reading and Understanding

Directions: Study the time line that shows important events leading up to the American Revolution. Then answer questions 1–5.

Events Leading to the American Revolution

The Intolerable Acts are passed to punish the colonies.

Delegates from almost all colonies meet at Continental Congress and boycott all goods from England.

Delegates advise Bostonians not to honor the Intolerable Acts.

Parliament passes the Stamp Act, which meets with the cry: "Taxation without representation!"	The Townshend Acts are passed.	The Boston Massacre occurs.	People protest during the Boston Tea Party.	
1765	1767	1770	1773	1774

---

1. **When does the time line show that people cried, "Taxation without representation!"?**
   - (A) after the Boston Massacre
   - (B) during the Continental Congress
   - (C) after the Stamp Act was passed
   - (D) during the fifth decade of the 1700s

2. **Of all the events listed, these events occurred closest together in time.**
   - (F) Townshend Acts; boycott of English goods
   - (G) advice not to honor the Intolerable Acts; Stamp Act
   - (H) passage of the Intolerable Acts; Boston Tea Party
   - (J) Stamp Act; Townshend Acts

3. **Which of these events happened first?**
   - (A) Boston Tea Party
   - (B) Townshend Acts
   - (C) Boston Massacre
   - (D) Stamp Act

4. **What period of time does this time line cover?**
   - (F) slightly less than one decade
   - (G) slightly more than one decade
   - (H) approximately one century
   - (J) about one millennium

5. **Which of the following events happened last?**
   - (A) The Stamp Act was passed.
   - (B) The Intolerable Acts were passed.
   - (C) The Boston Massacre occurred.
   - (D) People protested during the Boston Tea Party.

Name _____   Date_____

SOCIAL STUDIES
SAMPLE TEST

● **Directions:** Read each of the following carefully. Then mark the letter of the correct answer.

Examples

A. **Which of these states does not border the Mississippi River?**

- (A) Illinois
- (B) Kansas
- (C) Iowa
- (D) Minnesota

B. **In which time zone is Georgia located?**

- (F) eastern
- (G) central
- (H) mountain
- (J) pacific

---

1. **Which President sent Meriwether Lewis and William Clark on an expedition to explore the West?**

- (A) George Washington
- (B) John Tyler
- (C) Thomas Jefferson
- (D) Ulysses S. Grant

2. **How did Thomas Jefferson and James Madison try to change British action prior to 1812?**

- (F) through strong military force
- (G) through economic sanctions
- (H) through writing letters and sending official documents
- (J) through a laissez-faire policy

3. **Which was a major cause of the War of 1812?**

- (A) glutting the market with foreign goods
- (B) enacting railroad strikes
- (C) interfering with sailing routes
- (D) placing an embargo on crops

4. **Which of the following was not a major result of the Industrial Revolution in the United States?**

- (F) electricity
- (G) completion of modern transportation and communication systems
- (H) westward expansion
- (J) application of science to industrial workings and new products

5. **Who among the following opposed declaration of war in the War of 1812?**

- (A) farmers
- (B) Thomas Jefferson
- (C) James Madison
- (D) New Englanders

6. **Who among the following is not associated with the American Industrial Revolution?**

- (F) Bette Nesmith Graham and liquid paper
- (G) Eli Whitney and the cotton gin
- (H) James Watt and the steam engine
- (J) Samuel F. B. Morse and the telegraph

GO ON

Name _____   Date _____

For numbers 7–9, read the passage and answer the questions that follow.

Civil War Causes

It is widely held that slavery was the cause of the U.S. Civil War, though some have put forth the theory that the economic disparity between the North and South may have also been a cause.

Some experts say that a major cause of the Civil War was political action. Their theory states that political candidates seeking election used the issue of slavery to stir up political sentiment and catapult themselves into office.

Many experts believe that a mixture of causes brought about the Civil War. It is clear that the South's economy focused on agriculture, while the North was racing along with an eye on industrialization. This difference certainly could have contributed to the causes of the Civil War, but it is not the only cause of the war.

In the final analysis, many historians believe that not only slavery, but on a deeper level, the issues that led to differences of opinion about slavery, also caused the Civil War.

7. **Explain how the economic differences between the North and South are considred as one of the causes of the Civil War.**

    _____

    _____

    _____

8. **How did slavery and the opinions related to slavery become one of the major causes of the Civil War?**

    _____

    _____

    _____

9. **How can some historians say that politics was one of the causes of the Civil War?**

    _____

    _____

    _____

ANSWER SHEET

STUDENT'S NAME		
LAST	FIRST	MI

A	A	A	A	A	A	A	A	A	A	A	A	A	A	A	A	A	A
B	B	B	B	B	B	B	B	B	B	B	B	B	B	B	B	B	B
C	C	C	C	C	C	C	C	C	C	C	C	C	C	C	C	C	C
D	D	D	D	D	D	D	D	D	D	D	D	D	D	D	D	D	D
E	E	E	E	E	E	E	E	E	E	E	E	E	E	E	E	E	E
F	F	F	F	F	F	F	F	F	F	F	F	F	F	F	F	F	F
G	G	G	G	G	G	G	G	G	G	G	G	G	G	G	G	G	G
H	H	H	H	H	H	H	H	H	H	H	H	H	H	H	H	H	H
I	I	I	I	I	I	I	I	I	I	I	I	I	I	I	I	I	I
J	J	J	J	J	J	J	J	J	J	J	J	J	J	J	J	J	J
K	K	K	K	K	K	K	K	K	K	K	K	K	K	K	K	K	K
L	L	L	L	L	L	L	L	L	L	L	L	L	L	L	L	L	L
M	M	M	M	M	M	M	M	M	M	M	M	M	M	M	M	M	M
N	N	N	N	N	N	N	N	N	N	N	N	N	N	N	N	N	N
O	O	O	O	O	O	O	O	O	O	O	O	O	O	O	O	O	O
P	P	P	P	P	P	P	P	P	P	P	P	P	P	P	P	P	P
Q	Q	Q	Q	Q	Q	Q	Q	Q	Q	Q	Q	Q	Q	Q	Q	Q	Q
R	R	R	R	R	R	R	R	R	R	R	R	R	R	R	R	R	R
S	S	S	S	S	S	S	S	S	S	S	S	S	S	S	S	S	S
T	T	T	T	T	T	T	T	T	T	T	T	T	T	T	T	T	T
U	U	U	U	U	U	U	U	U	U	U	U	U	U	U	U	U	U
V	V	V	V	V	V	V	V	V	V	V	V	V	V	V	V	V	V
W	W	W	W	W	W	W	W	W	W	W	W	W	W	W	W	W	W
X	X	X	X	X	X	X	X	X	X	X	X	X	X	X	X	X	X
Y	Y	Y	Y	Y	Y	Y	Y	Y	Y	Y	Y	Y	Y	Y	Y	Y	Y
Z	Z	Z	Z	Z	Z	Z	Z	Z	Z	Z	Z	Z	Z	Z	Z	Z	Z

SCHOOL

TEACHER

FEMALE ◯ MALE ◯

BIRTH DATE				
MONTH	DAY		YEAR	
JAN ◯	0	0		0
FEB ◯	1	1		1
MAR ◯	2	2		2
APR ◯	3	3		3
MAY ◯		4		4
JUN ◯		5	5	5
JUL ◯		6	6	6
AUG ◯		7	7	7
SEP ◯		8	8	8
OCT ◯		9	9	9
NOV ◯			0	
DEC ◯				

GRADE

7 8 9

Part 1: SOCIAL STUDIES

A	A B C D	**5**	A B C D	**10**	F G H J	**15**	A B C D
1	A B C D	**6**	F G H J	**11**	A B C D	**16**	F G H J
2	F G H J	**7**	A B C D	**12**	F G H J	**17**	A B C D
3	A B C D	**8**	F G H J	**13**	A B C D	**18**	F G H J
4	F G H J	**9**	A B C D	**14**	F G H J		

Name _____ Date _____

SOCIAL STUDIES: PRACTICE TEST

Directions: Read each statement carefully. Then mark the letter that corresponds to the correct answer.

Example

A. The number of amendments to the Constitution is—

- (A) 10.
- (B) 21.
- (C) 27.
- (D) 34.

1. **Presidential elections are held during this month.**
    - (A) April
    - (B) January
    - (C) November
    - (D) December

2. **Which of these documents did the Constitution replace?**
    - (F) Statement of Human Rights
    - (G) Bill of Rights
    - (H) Articles of Confederation
    - (J) Mayflower Compact

3. **He is referred to as the "Father of the Constitution."**
    - (A) George Washington
    - (B) Benjamin Franklin
    - (C) James Madison
    - (D) Samuel Adams

4. **Which of these cities was the setting for the famous midnight ride of Paul Revere?**
    - (F) Philadelphia
    - (G) Concord
    - (H) Boston
    - (J) New York City

5. **Charges of impeachment can be brought against the president by—**
    - (A) Congress.
    - (B) The House of Representatives.
    - (C) The Senate.
    - (D) The Vice President.

6. **The system outlined within the Constitution to prevent an abuse of power by any governing body is called—**
    - (F) colonial legislation.
    - (G) the bill of rights.
    - (H) checks and balances.
    - (J) President's Cabinet.

7. **He became president when President Kennedy was assassinated.**
    - (A) Lyndon Johnson
    - (B) Calvin Coolidge
    - (C) Theodore Roosevelt
    - (D) Richard Nixon

8. **Which of these presidents was not assassinated while in office?**
    - (F) Abraham Lincoln
    - (G) James A. Garfield
    - (H) William McKinley
    - (J) Ronald Reagan

GO ON

Name _____   Date_____

⬛ SOCIAL STUDIES PRACTICE TEST ⬛

9. How many presidents have been impeached?
   - (A) 1
   - (B) 2
   - (C) 3
   - (D) 4

10. The river that flows from north to south dividing the nation in half.
    - (F) Missouri
    - (G) Mississippi
    - (H) Ohio
    - (J) Allegheny

11. Which of these presidents does not have his portrait appearing on a coin?
    - (A) George Washington
    - (B) Abraham Lincoln
    - (C) Theodore Roosevelt
    - (D) Thomas Jefferson

12. This crop turned out to be the savior of the colony of Virginia.
    - (F) corn
    - (G) indigo
    - (H) tobacco
    - (J) rice

13. The Louisiana Territory, which virtually doubled the size of the United States, was bought from—
    - (A) Spain.
    - (B) France.
    - (C) Great Britain.
    - (D) Canada.

14. Which of the following is not addressed in the first ten amendments to the Constitution?
    - (F) freedom of speech
    - (G) right to bear arms
    - (H) abolition of slavery
    - (J) right against unreasonable search and seizure

15. Who played the major role in drafting the Declaration of Independence?
    - (A) Thomas Jefferson
    - (B) Benjamin Franklin
    - (C) John Hancock
    - (D) John Adams

16. Who among the following did not participate in the drafting or signing of the Declaration of Independence?
    - (F) Roger Sherman
    - (G) Robert Livingston
    - (H) James Madison
    - (J) Grover Cleveland

17. The goal of the abolitionist movement was—
    - (A) to end slavery.
    - (B) to promote agricultural progress.
    - (C) to slow down industry.
    - (D) to influence the Continental Congress.

18. Which body of water is nearest Louisiana?
    - (F) Atlantic Ocean
    - (G) Pacific Ocean
    - (H) Gulf of Mexico
    - (J) Bering Sea

GO ON ⟩

SOCIAL STUDIES PRACTICE TEST

Read the following passage. Then answer questions 19–21.

Bill of Rights

The men who wrote the original Constitution did not think it was necessary to list the individual rights of the people. They assumed that because the various state constitutions contained lists of individual rights, it should not be necessary to place them in the U.S. Constitution. When copies of the new Constitution were dispatched to the states and the people for a "first look," they found out differently.

There was an overwhelming insistence among the people that individual rights of men and women should be spelled out. Such was the condition under which several of the state conventions ratified the Constitution. They would ratify the document only if a bill of rights would be added. Congress was quick to comply.

The Constitution went into effect in 1789. In that same year, Congress reviewed more than twenty amendments suggested by the ratifying conventions. Congress pared the list down to twelve, which were submitted to the states to be ratified. Ten of them were approved and became part of the Constitution by 1791.

Because they followed so soon after the original document, they are looked at historically as almost being a part of the original document. But they clearly point to one of the first major uses of the Constitution as the framework of the American nation—namely, the process involved in changing it to suit the needs of the people. These first ten amendments also point to the power of the people themselves to make certain that their own liberties were not overlooked.

The people wanted their rights protected, too. They got their wish in the form of the first ten amendments, known as the Bill of Rights.

19. Describe the Bill of Rights in a sentence.

_____

_____

20. Explain why the people insisted that a bill of rights be added to the Constitution.

_____

_____

21. Explain why the men who wrote the Constitution did not include a bill of rights in the original document.

_____

_____

ANSWER KEY

READING: VOCABULARY
Lesson 1: Synonyms
• Page 11
- A. A
- B. G
- 1. C
- 2. J
- 3. C
- 4. H
- 5. B
- 6. J
- 7. A
- 8. H

READING: VOCABULARY
Lesson 2: Antonyms
• Page 12
- A. A
- B. G
- 1. D
- 2. H
- 3. D
- 4. H
- 5. A
- 6. H
- 7. D
- 8. G

READING: VOCABULARY
Lesson 3: Multi-Meaning Words
• Page 13
- A. A
- B. H
- 1. D
- 2. G
- 3. A
- 4. G
- 5. D
- 6. H

READING: VOCABULARY
Lesson 4: Words in Context
• Page 14
- A. B
- B. F
- 1. C
- 2. H
- 3. D
- 4. F
- 5. B
- 6. J

READING: VOCABULARY
Sample Test
• Page 15
- A. C
- B. F
- 1. C
- 2. H
- 3. C
- 4. F
- 5. B
- 6. J
- 7. B
- 8. G
- 9. B
- 10. F
- 11. B
- 12. J
- 13. B
- 14. F
- 15. D

- 16. G
- 17. C
- 18. F

READING: COMPREHENSION
Lesson 5: Main Idea
• Page 17
- A. C
- 1. B
- 2. G
- 3. A

READING: COMPREHENSION
Lesson 6: Recalling Details
• Page 18
- A. B
- 1. B
- 2. F
- 3. C

READING: COMPREHENSION
Lesson 7: Inferences
• Page 19
- A. A
- 1. C
- 2. G

READING: COMPREHENSION
Lesson 8: Fact and Opinion/Drawing Conclusions
• Page 20
- A. C
- 1. D

READING: COMPREHENSION
Lesson 9: Story Elements
• Page 21
- A. B
- 1. C
- 2. G
- 3. D

READING: COMPREHENSION
Lesson 10: Nonfiction
• Pages 22–23
- A. C
- 1. D
- 2. H
- 3. A
- 4. F
- 5. A
- 6. G
- 7. C

READING: COMPREHENSION
Lesson 11: Nonfiction
• Pages 24–25
- A. B
- 1. B
- 2. H
- 3. A
- 4. J
- 5. C
- 6. G

READING: COMPREHENSION
Lesson 12: Nonfiction
• Pages 26–27
- A. A
- 1. C
- 2. G
- 3. C
- 4. G
- 5. D
- 6. F
- 7. B

READING: COMPREHENSION
Lesson 13: Fiction
• Pages 28–29
- A. C
- 1. A
- 2. J
- 3. A
- 4. F
- 5. C
- 6. G
- 7. A

READING: COMPREHENSION
Lesson 14: Fiction
• Pages 30–31
- A. B
- 1. C
- 2. J
- 3. A
- 4. J
- 5. C
- 6. J
- 7. D

READING: COMPREHENSION
Lesson 15: Fiction
• Pages 32–33
- A. B
- 1. C
- 2. F
- 3. B
- 4. J
- 5. A
- 6. J
- 7. C

READING: COMPREHENSION
Sample Test
• Pages 34–38
- A. D
- 1. A
- 2. H
- 3. B
- 4. F
- 5. D
- 6. G
- 7. B
- 8. J
- 9. A
- 10. H
- 11. A
- 12. G
- 13. D
- 14. G
- 15. C
- 16. J

READING: PRACTICE TEST
Part 1: Vocabulary
• Pages 40–43
- A. C
- B. F
- 1. C
- 2. H
- 3. A
- 4. G
- 5. D
- 6. F
- 7. B
- 8. G
- 9. D
- 10. F
- 11. A

12. G
13. D
14. F
15. B
16. J
17. B
18. H
19. A
20. J
21. B
22. J
23. A
24. G
25. A
26. J
27. C
28. H
29. D
30. G
31. B
32. H

READING: PRACTICE TEST
Part 2: Comprehension
• Pages 44–47
A. B
1. D
2. H
3. B
4. F
5. D
6. H
7. A
8. G
9. B
10. F
11. D
12. G
13. B
14. H

LANGUAGE: MECHANICS
Lesson 1: Punctuation
• Pages 48–49
A. D
B. H
1. D
2. F
3. B
4. J
5. B
6. F
7. D
8. F
9. A
10. J
11. C
12. J
13. C
14. H
15. B
16. F
17. B

LANGUAGE: MECHANICS
AND PUNCTUATION
Lesson 2: Capitalization
• Pages 50–52
A. A
B. J
1. C

2. J
3. C
4. J
5. A
6. J
7. C
8. F
9. C
10. F
11. B
12. F
13. D
14. H
15. A
16. F
17. C
18. F
19. A
20. F
21. A
22. F
23. D
24. F

LANGUAGE: MECHANICS
Sample Test
• Pages 53–54
A. C
1. D
2. F
3. A
4. H
5. A
6. F
7. C
8. F
9. C
10. H
11. D
12. F
13. D
14. J
15. A

LANGUAGE: EXPRESSION
Lesson 3: Usage
• Pages 55–57
A. D
B. G
1. B
2. H
3. A
4. F
5. D
6. G
7. D
8. G
9. A
10. H
11. A
12. J
13. D
14. F
15. D
16. H
17. D
18. G
19. D
20. H

LANGUAGE: EXPRESSION
Lesson 4: Sentences
• Pages 58–60
A. A
B. F
1. A
2. F
3. B
4. H
5. C
6. G
7. C
8. H
9. C
10. G
11. A
12. F
13. A
14. G
15. D

LANGUAGE: EXPRESSION
Lesson 5: Paragraphs
• Pages 61–64
A. B
1. D
2. G
3. D
4. F
5. B
6. H
7. B
8. J
9. A
10. H
11. B
12. F
13. B
14. J

LANGUAGE: EXPRESSION
Sample Test
• Pages 65–68
A. B
1. C
2. G
3. D
4. J
5. B
6. G
7. B
8. G
9. B
10. G
11. A
12. J
13. D
14. H
15. C
16. F
17. A
18. J
19. D
20. J

LANGUAGE: SPELLING
Lesson 6: Spelling Skills
• Pages 69–70
A. B
B. G
1. C

2. J
3. D
4. H
5. C
6. F
7. D
8. G
9. D
10. F
11. A
12. J
13. D
14. J
15. B
16. F
17. C

LANGUAGE: SPELLING
Spelling Test
• Pages 71–72
A. C
B. H
1. A
2. H
3. B
4. G
5. D
6. J
7. C
8. H
9. A
10. J
11. B
12. F
13. D
14. G
15. C
16. H
17. A
18. J
19. D

LANGUAGE: STUDY SKILLS
Lesson 7: Study Skills
• Pages 73–75
A. C
1. C
2. G
3. D
4. F
5. A
6. G
7. C
8. H
9. A
10. G
11. C
12. J
13. A
14. H
15. B
16. H
17. D
18. F
19. A
20. G

LANGUAGE: STUDY SKILLS
Sample Test
• Pages 76–78
A. C

B. H
1. D
2. F
3. B
4. G
5. C
6. G
7. A
8. H
9. C
10. H
11. A
12. H
13. C
14. J
15. C
16. H
17. C
18. G

LANGUAGE: PRACTICE TEST
Part 1: Mechanics
• Pages 80–82
A. C
1. C
2. J
3. B
4. G
5. B
6. G
7. D
8. H
9. B
10. G
11. D
12. H
13. A
14. J
15. C
16. H
17. A
18. G
19. B
20. G
21. C

LANGUAGE: PRACTICE TEST
Part 2: Expression
• Pages 83–85
A. D
1. D
2. J
3. D
4. G
5. D
6. G
7. C
8. H
9. A
10. H
11. A
12. F
13. B
14. J
15. D
16. G

LANGUAGE: PRACTICE TEST
Part 3: Spelling
• Pages 86–87
A. C

B. F
1. A
2. H
3. C
4. G
5. D
6. H
7. A
8. F
9. D
10. H
11. D
12. H
13. C
14. F
15. B
16. J
17. B
18. J
19. B

LANGUAGE: PRACTICE TEST
Part 4: Study Skills
• Pages 88–89
A. C
1. C
2. H
3. B
4. J
5. C
6. H
7. C
8. J
9. C
10. H

MATH: CONCEPTS
Lesson 1: Numeration
• Pages 90–92
A. B
B. J
1. B
2. F
3. D
4. G
5. B
6. G
7. D
8. G
9. B
10. F
11. D
12. F
13. B
14. H
15. B
16. H
17. C
18. G
19. B
20. H
21. C
22. G
23. C
24. H

MATH: CONCEPTS
Lesson 2: Number Concepts
• Pages 93–95

A. C
B. F
1. B
2. H
3. C
4. F
5. B
6. H
7. B
8. H
9. D
10. F
11. C
12. J
13. D
14. H
15. C
16. G
17. B
18. F
19. A
20. J
21. C

MATH: CONCEPTS
Lesson 3: Fractions and Decimals
• Pages 96–98

A. D
B. F
1. B
2. F
3. B
4. H
5. D
6. J
7. C
8. J
9. B
10. G
11. A
12. F
13. D
14. H
15. C
16. H
17. A
18. J
19. B
20. J
21. D
22. H

MATH: CONCEPTS
Sample Test
• Pages 99–101

A. A
B. G
1. C
2. H
3. C
4. J
5. D
6. J
7. C
8. H
9. C
10. H

11. B
12. H
13. B
14. G
15. B
16. F
17. C
18. G
19. D
20. G
21. B
22. F
23. C
24. J

MATH: COMPUTATION
Lesson 4: Whole Numbers
• Pages 102–103

A. B
B. C
1. C
2. F
3. D
4. G
5. B
6. F
7. D
8. G
9. A
10. J
11. B
12. F
13. C
14. G
15. B
16. F
17. C

MATH: COMPUTATION
Lesson 5: Decimals
• Pages 104–105

A. C
B. J
1. B
2. F
3. D
4. F
5. C
6. F
7. B
8. H
9. C
10. G
11. D
12. G
13. A
14. F
15. A
16. F
17. A

MATH: COMPUTATION
Lesson 6: Percent
• Pages 106–107

A. B
B. G
1. A
2. G
3. D
4. F
5. C

6. H
7. B
8. G
9. C
10. G
11. A
12. H
13. C
14. H
15. A
16. H
17. B

MATH: COMPUTATION
Lesson 7: Fractions
• Pages 108–109

A. C
B. F
1. C
2. F
3. A
4. H
5. D
6. J
7. B
8. G
9. B
10. H
11. A
12. H
13. C
14. F
15. D
16. G

MATH: COMPUTATION
Sample Test
• Pages 110–112

A. D
B. F
1. A
2. G
3. B
4. H
5. B
6. G
7. D
8. F
9. A
10. J
11. D
12. H
13. D
14. G
15. C
16. G
17. A
18. G
19. C
20. F
21. D
22. F
23. C
24. G

MATH: APPLICATIONS
Lesson 8: Geometry
· Pages 113–115
- A. C
- 1. C
- 2. H
- 3. B
- 4. H
- 5. B
- 6. G
- 7. D
- 8. J
- 9. B
- 10. H
- 11. D
- 12. H
- 13. A
- 14. H
- 15. A
- 16. G

MATH: APPLICATIONS
Lesson 9: Measurement
· Pages 116–117
- A. A
- 1. C
- 2. G
- 3. B
- 4. H
- 5. C
- 6. H
- 7. B
- 8. H
- 9. A
- 10. G
- 11. B
- 12. H
- 13. C
- 14. G
- 15. A

MATH: APPLICATIONS
Lesson 10: Problem Solving
· Pages 118–120
- A. B
- B. G
- 1. B
- 2. G
- 3. D
- 4. G
- 5. C
- 6. G
- 7. A
- 8. H
- 9. D
- 10. H
- 11. B
- 12. J
- 13. C
- 14. F
- 15. B
- 16. J

MATH: APPLICATIONS
Lesson 11: Algebra
· Pages 121–122
- A. D
- B. F
- 1. B
- 2. J
- 3. D

- 4. G
- 5. C
- 6. G
- 7. D
- 8. H
- 9. A
- 10. G
- 11. B
- 12. H

MATH: APPLICATIONS
Sample Test
· Pages 123–126
- A. B
- B. G
- 1. C
- 2. J
- 3. D
- 4. G
- 5. C
- 6. G
- 7. B
- 8. G
- 9. C
- 10. F
- 11. B
- 12. H
- 13. D
- 14. H
- 15. D
- 16. F
- 17. C
- 18. G
- 19. C
- 20. G
- 21. C
- 22. J
- 23. B
- 24. F
- 25. C
- 26. G

MATH: PRACTICE TEST
Part 1: Concepts
· Pages 128–129
- A. A
- B. J
- 1. C
- 2. G
- 3. A
- 4. H
- 5. C
- 6. F
- 7. B
- 8. G
- 9. C
- 10. J
- 11. B
- 12. G
- 13. A
- 14. J
- 15. C
- 16. J
- 17. B

MATH: PRACTICE TEST
Part 2: Computation
· Pages 130–131
- A. C
- B. F
- 1. B

- 2. F
- 3. C
- 4. H
- 5. B
- 6. J
- 7. C
- 8. H
- 9. B
- 10. J
- 11. A
- 12. J
- 13. C
- 14. F
- 15. B
- 16. J
- 17. A
- 18. G
- 19. A
- 20. H
- 21. D
- 22. J

MATH: PRACTICE TEST
Part 3: Applications
· Pages 132–133
- A. D
- B. J
- 1. B
- 2. G
- 3. B
- 4. G
- 5. A
- 6. H
- 7. A
- 8. H
- 9. C
- 10. G
- 11. C
- 12. F
- 13. B
- 14. G
- 15. C
- 16. H

SCIENCE
Lesson 1: General Knowledge
· Pages 134–136
- A. C
- 1. B
- 2. F
- 3. B
- 4. G
- 5. C
- 6. H
- 7. D
- 8. H
- 9. D
- 10. F
- 11. B
- 12. F
- 13. D
- 14. G
- 15. C
- 16. G
- 17. B
- 18. G
- 19. D
- 20. H
- 21. D
- 22. J

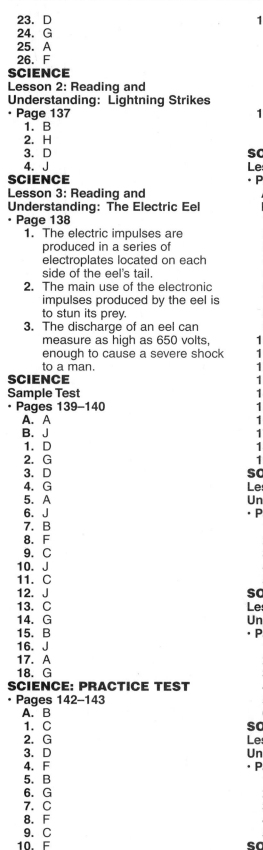

23. D
24. G
25. A
26. F

SCIENCE
Lesson 2: Reading and Understanding: Lightning Strikes
• Page 137
1. B
2. H
3. D
4. J

SCIENCE
Lesson 3: Reading and Understanding: The Electric Eel
• Page 138
1. The electric impulses are produced in a series of electroplates located on each side of the eel's tail.
2. The main use of the electronic impulses produced by the eel is to stun its prey.
3. The discharge of an eel can measure as high as 650 volts, enough to cause a severe shock to a man.

SCIENCE
Sample Test
• Pages 139–140
A. A
B. J
1. D
2. G
3. D
4. G
5. A
6. J
7. B
8. F
9. C
10. J
11. C
12. J
13. C
14. G
15. B
16. J
17. A
18. G

SCIENCE: PRACTICE TEST
• Pages 142–143
A. B
1. C
2. G
3. D
4. F
5. B
6. G
7. C
8. F
9. C
10. F
11. C
12. J
13. B
14. G

15. Animals with bilateral symmetry have matching body parts on either side of the center of their bodies, while animals with radial symmetry have body parts that radiate from the center like spokes in a wheel.
16. The eyes, ears, arms, and legs of a man are all examples of man's bilateral symmetry.

SOCIAL STUDIES
Lesson 1: General Knowledge
• Pages 144–145
A. D
B. F
1. B
2. H
3. D
4. G
5. A
6. G
7. D
8. F
9. A
10. G
11. B
12. J
13. C
14. F
15. D
16. G
17. C
18. H
19. A

SOCIAL STUDIES
Lesson 2: Reading and Understanding
• Page 146
1. B
2. F
3. B
4. G
5. C

SOCIAL STUDIES
Lesson 3: Reading and Understanding
• Page 147
1. C
2. F
3. B
4. F
5. B
6. H

SOCIAL STUDIES
Lesson 4: Reading and Understanding
• Page 148
1. C
2. H
3. D
4. F
5. B

SOCIAL STUDIES
Sample Test
• Pages 149–150
A. B
B. F
1. C

2. G
3. C
4. H
5. A
6. F
7. The economy of the North was focused on industrialization, while the economy of the South was based on agriculture.
8. Industrialists in the North were opposed to slavery primarily because it was of no advantage to them. Plantation owners in the South wanted slaves to work in their cotton fields.
9. Political candidates seeking election used the issue of slavery to stir up political turmoil in the hope of being elected.

SOCIAL STUDIES: PRACTICE TEST
• Pages 152–154
A. C
1. C
2. H
3. C
4. H
5. B
6. H
7. A
8. J
9. B
10. G
11. C
12. H
13. B
14. H
15. A
16. J
17. A
18. H
19. The Bill of Rights is a listing of the individual rights to which we are entitled.
20. The people had lost many of their basic human rights under the rule of England, and they were not about to allow that to happen under the new government.
21. The men who wrote the original Constitution felt that the rights of individuals were contained in the various state constitutions.